General Care of Horses

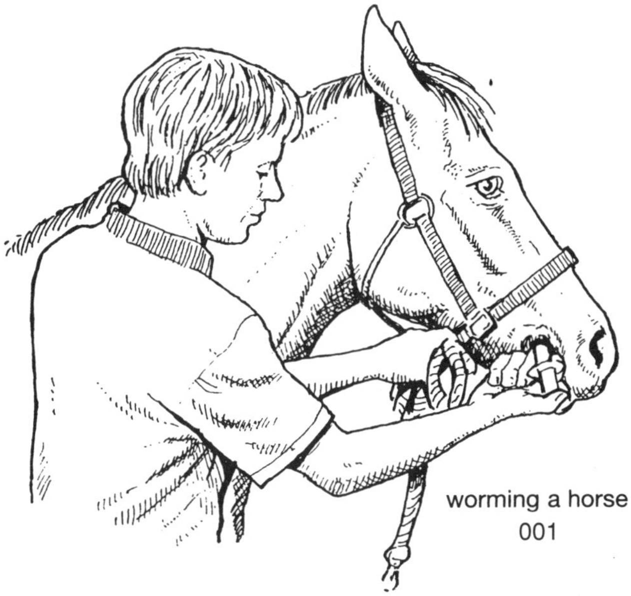

worming a horse
001

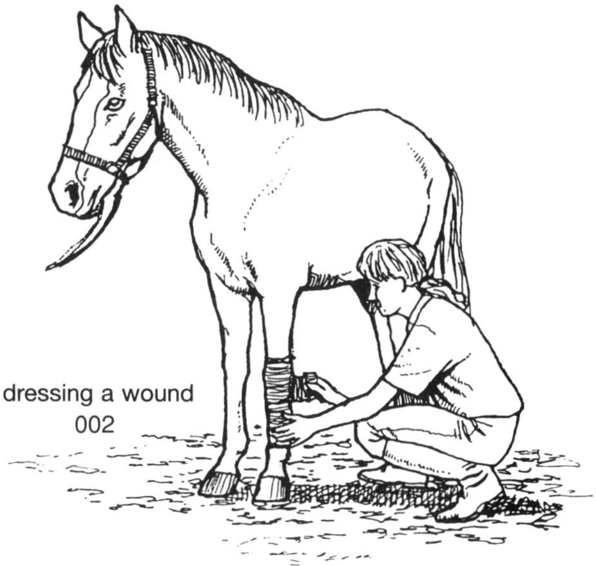

dressing a wound
002

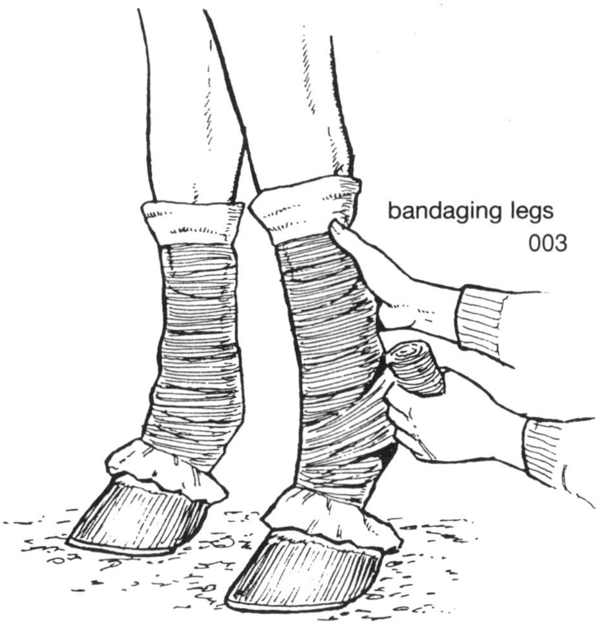

bandaging legs
003

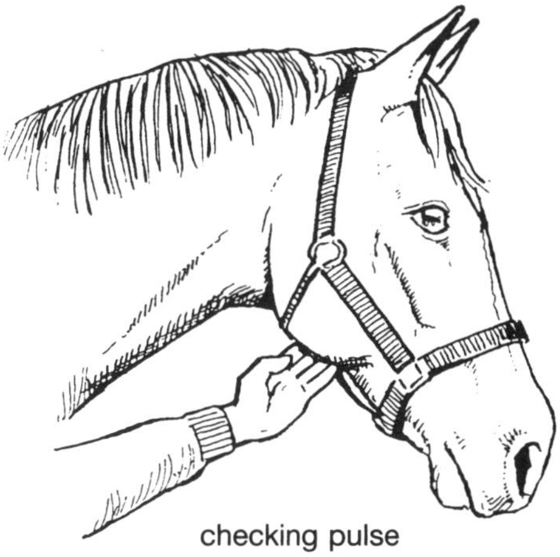

checking pulse
004

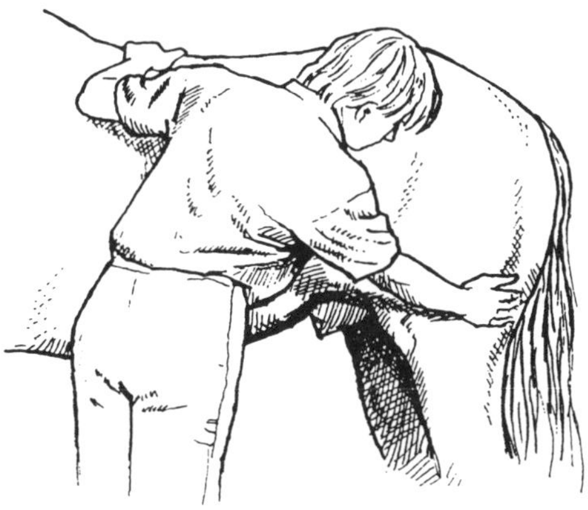

checking horse all over for signs of inflammation: heat, swelling, and pain
005

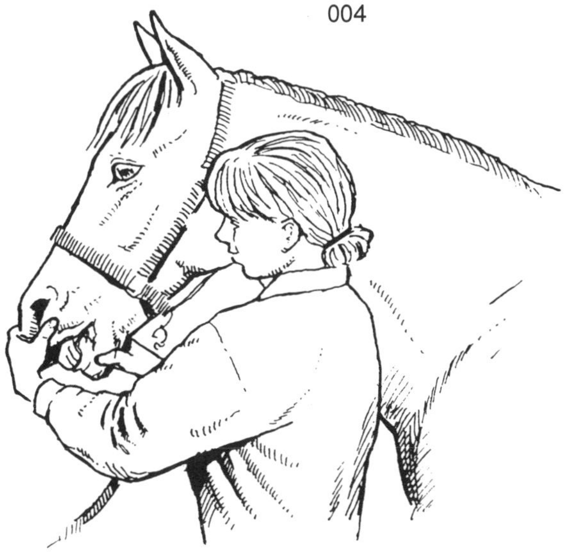

examining the mouth
006

General Care of Horses

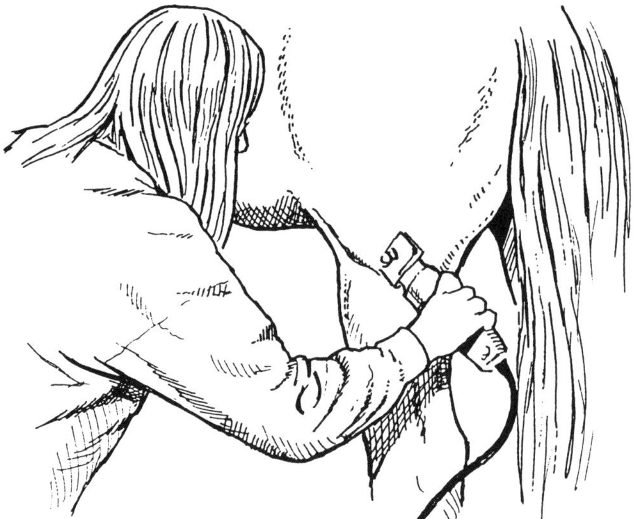

007

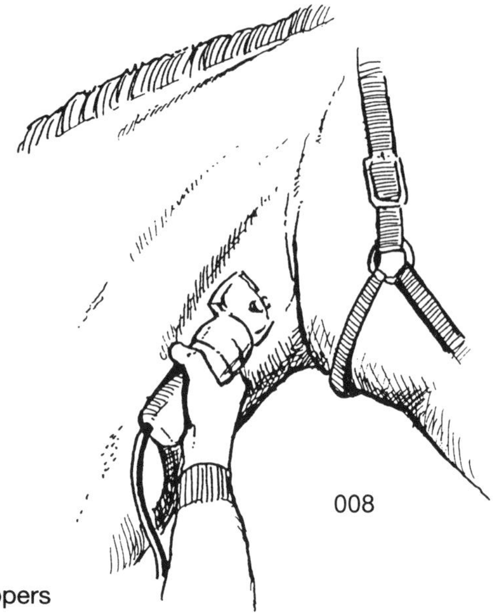

008

using clippers

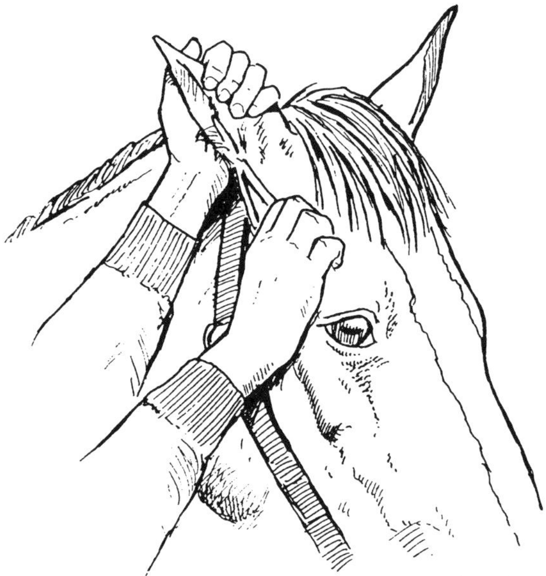

trimming ears

009

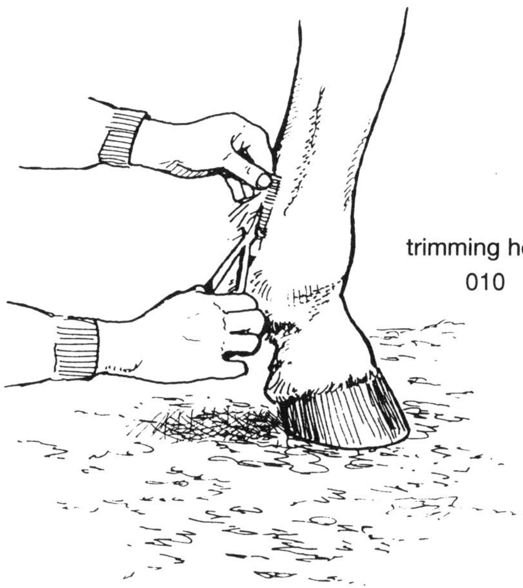

trimming heels

010

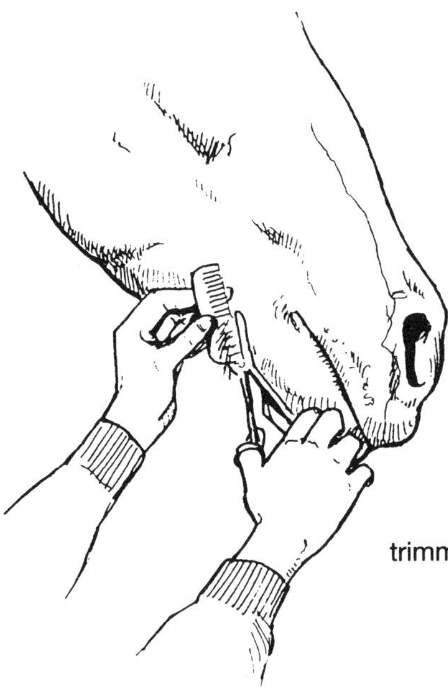

trimming face

011

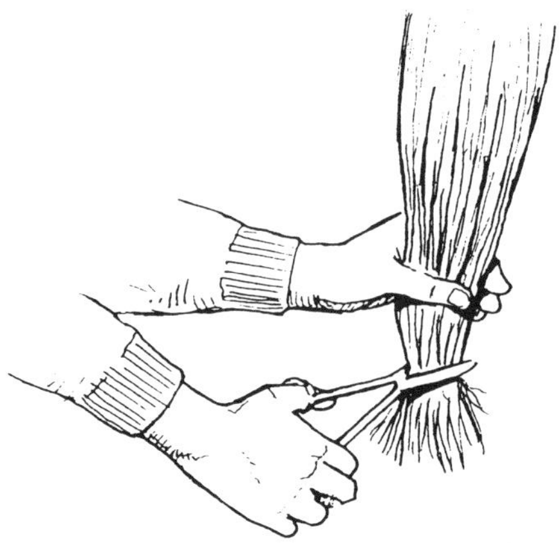

trimming tail

012

General Care of Horses

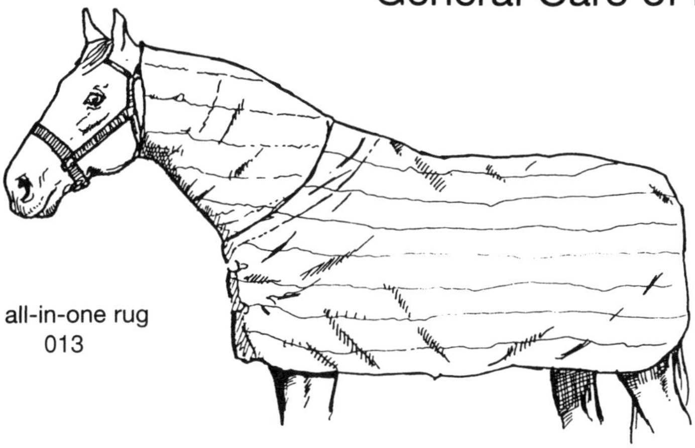

all-in-one rug
013

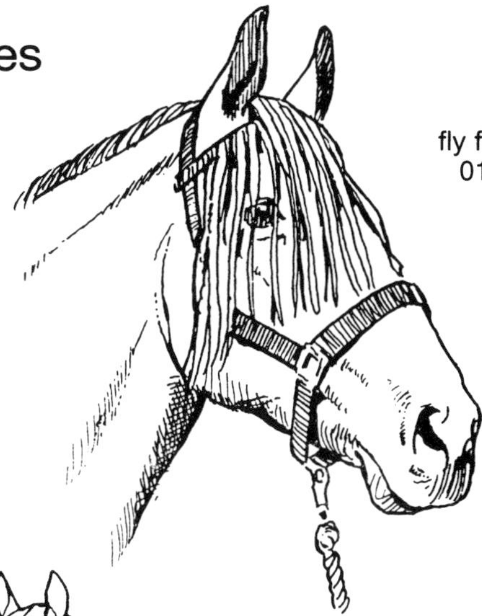

fly fringe
014

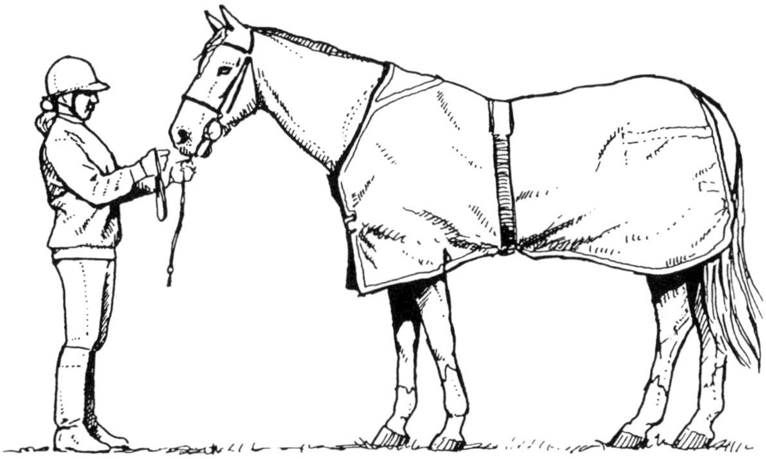

stable rug
015

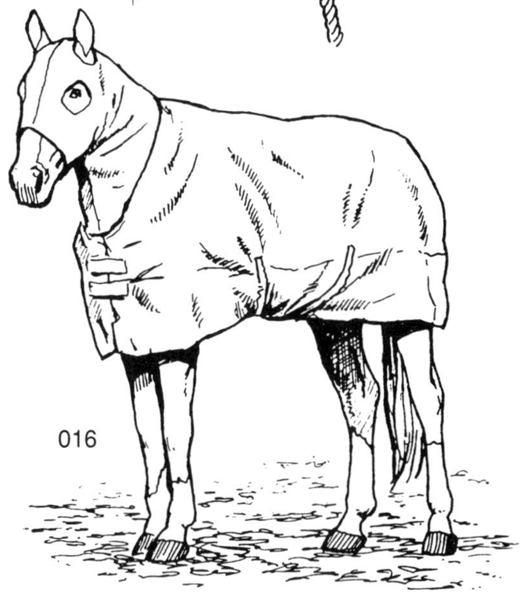

016

all-in-one rug for winter

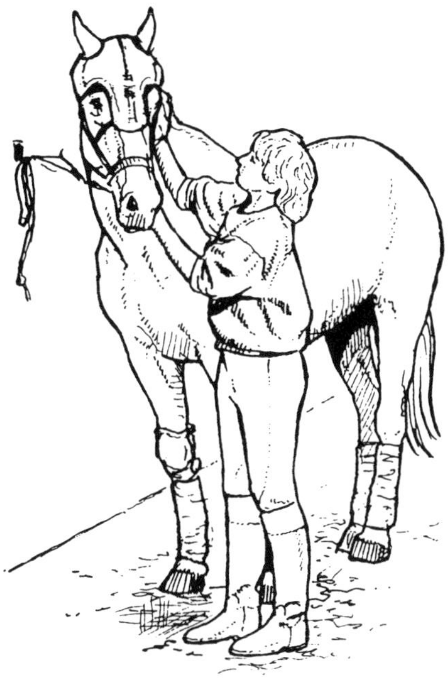

putting on protective headgear and
leg and knee boots
017

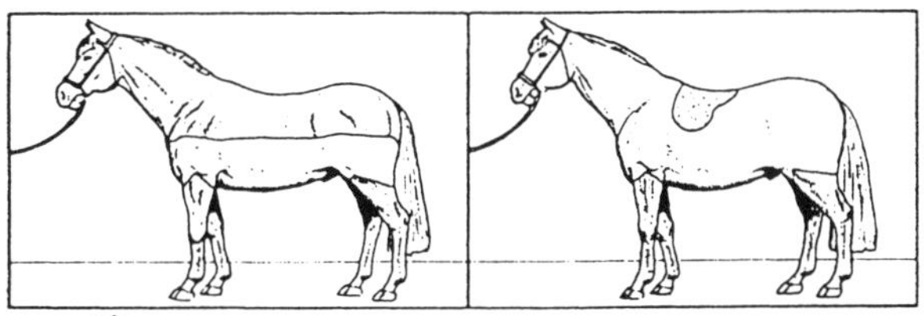

018

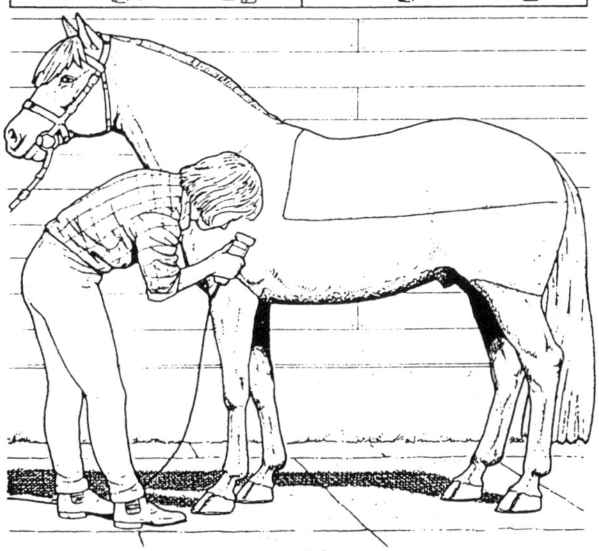

019

Types of Clip

trace clip, saddle or hunter clip, and blanket clip

Horse's Feet

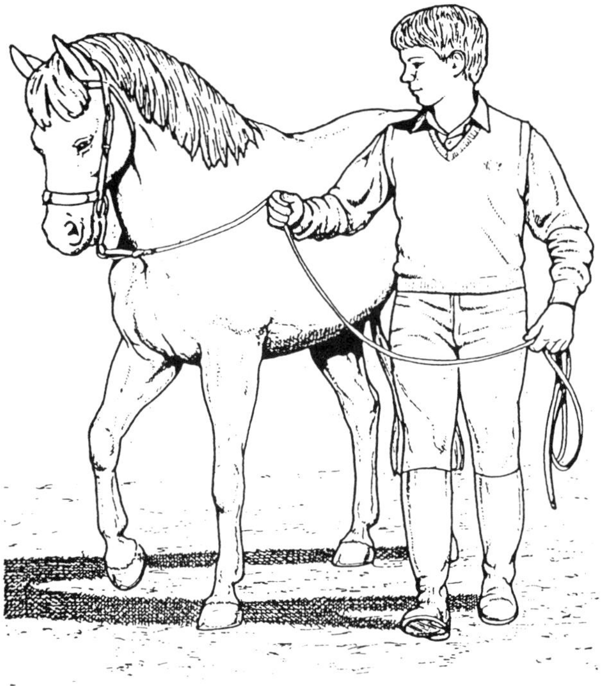

checking for lameness
020

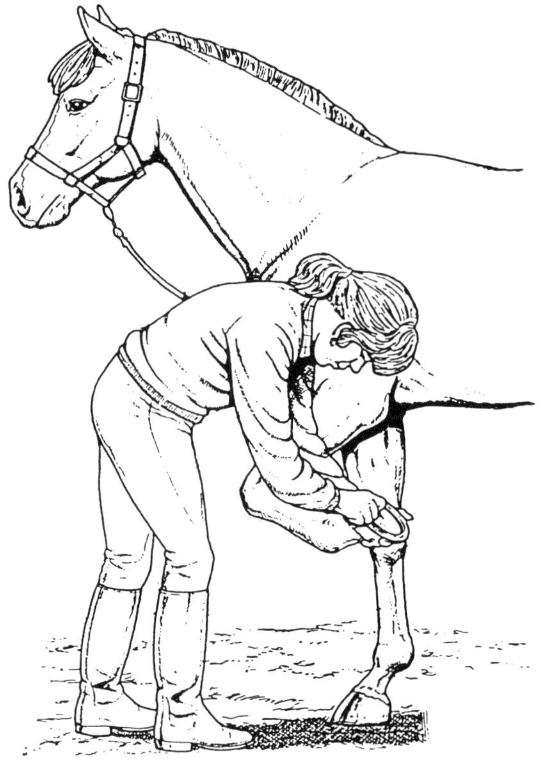

cleaning out feet
021

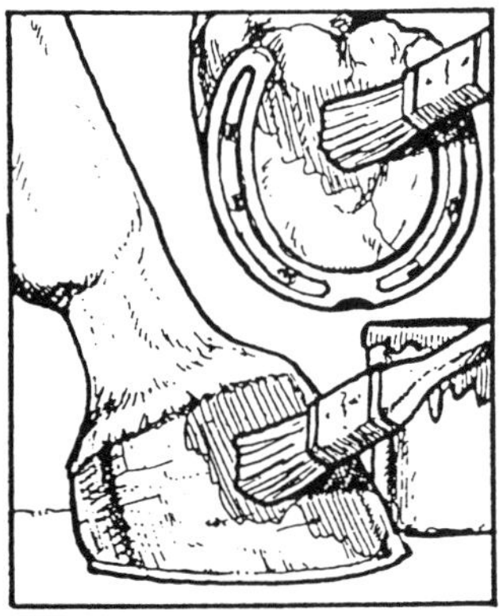

oiling and painting the hoof
022

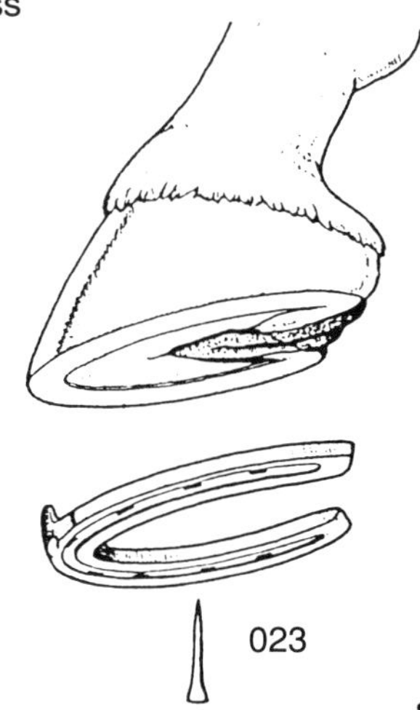

023
the horseshoe

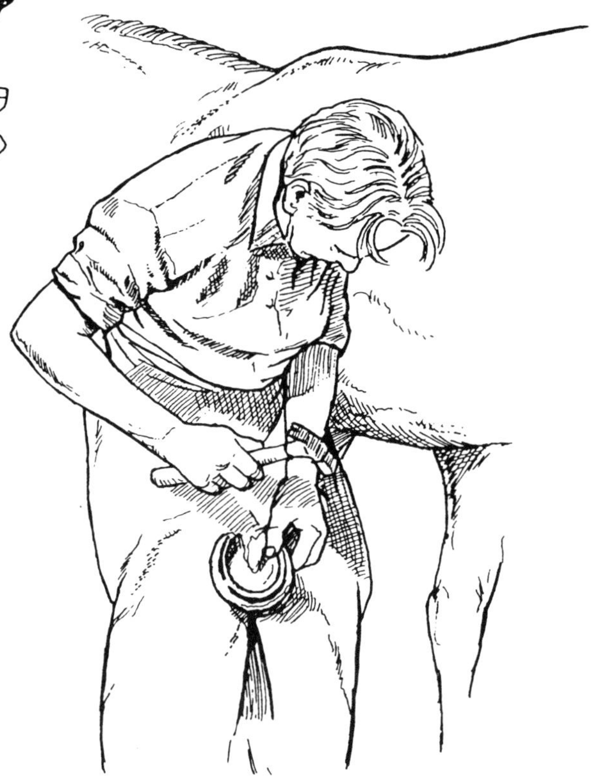

fitting new shoe
025

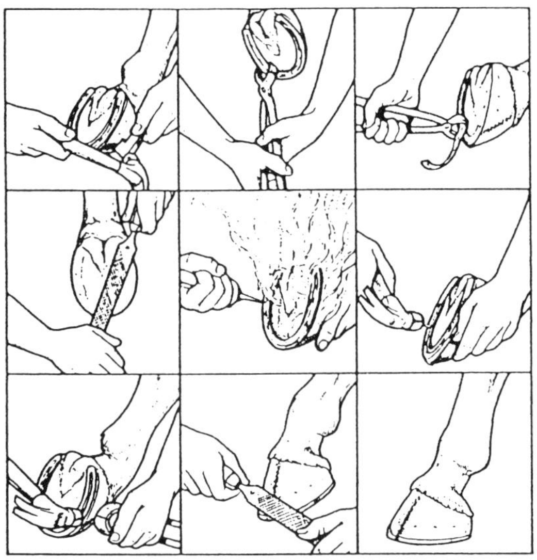

removing horseshoe
024

Grooming a Horse

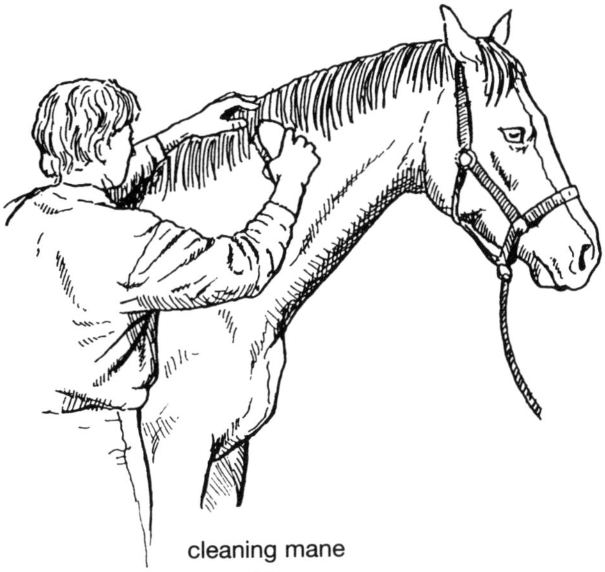

cleaning mane
026

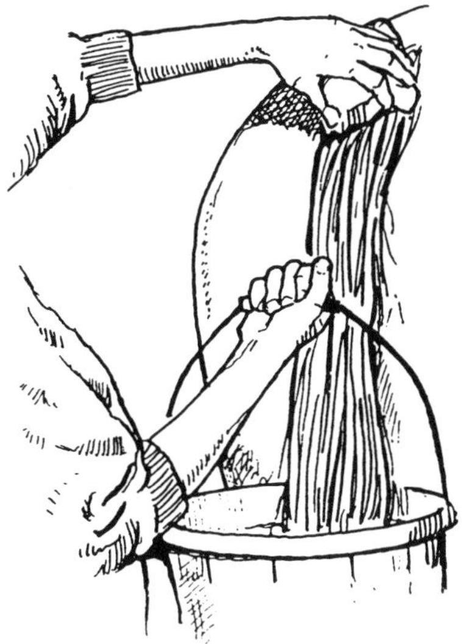

washing tail
027

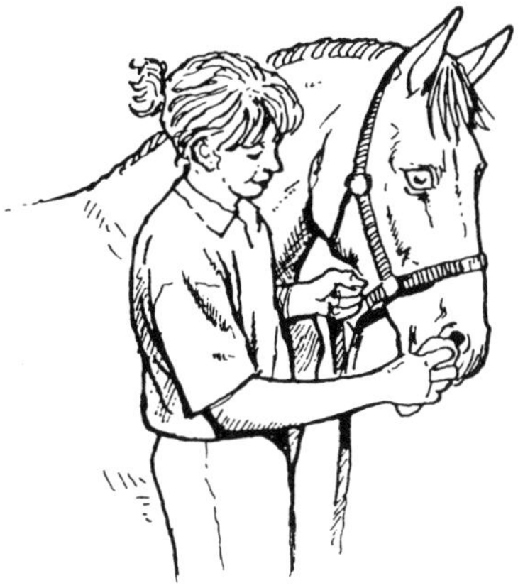

cleaning muzzle with soft sponge
028

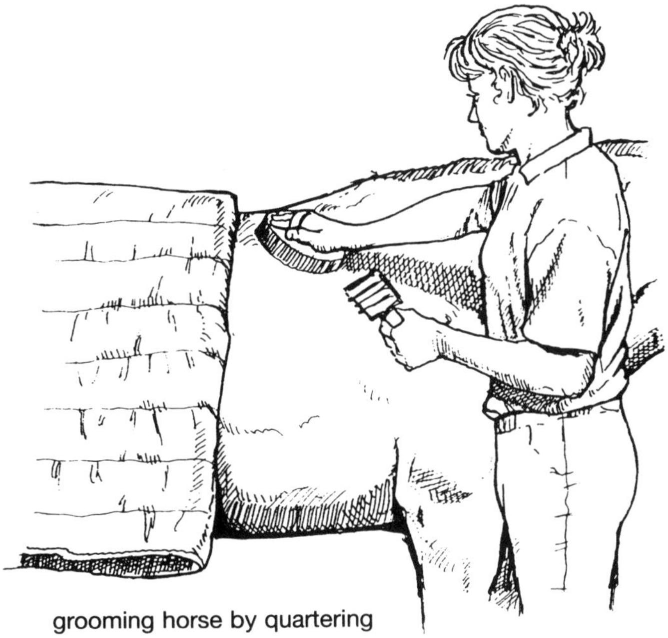

grooming horse by quartering
029

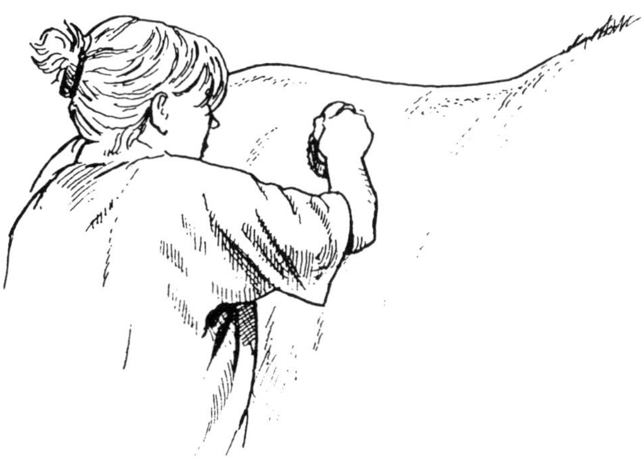

using a stable rubber
030

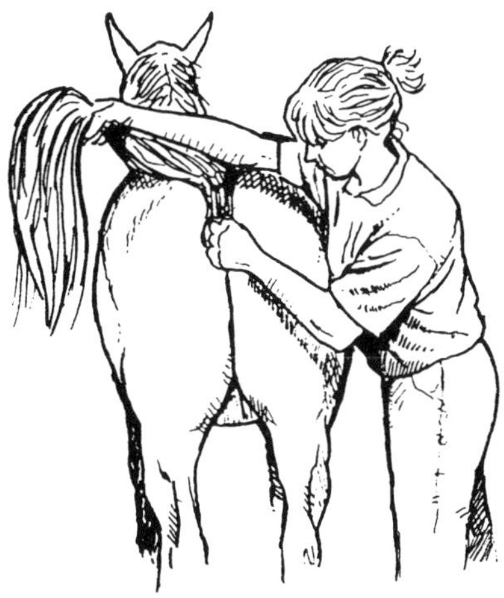

cleaning the dock
031

Grooming Horse—Preparing for a Show

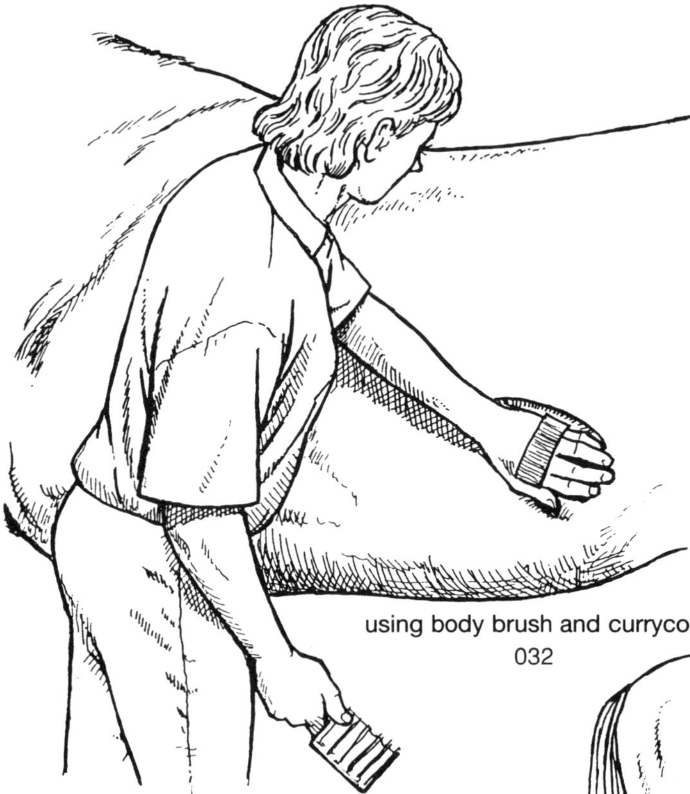

using body brush and currycomb
032

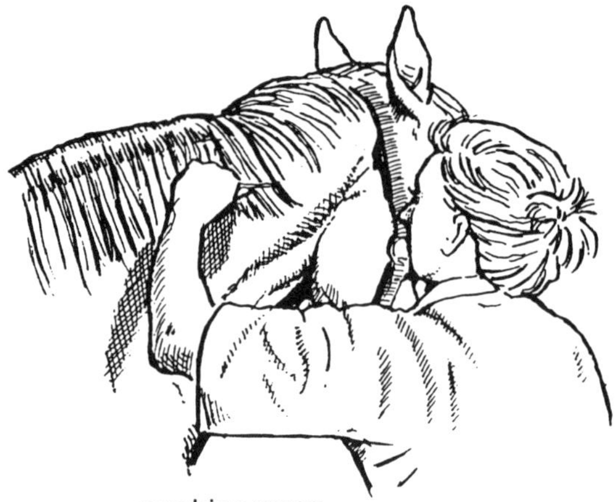

combing mane
033

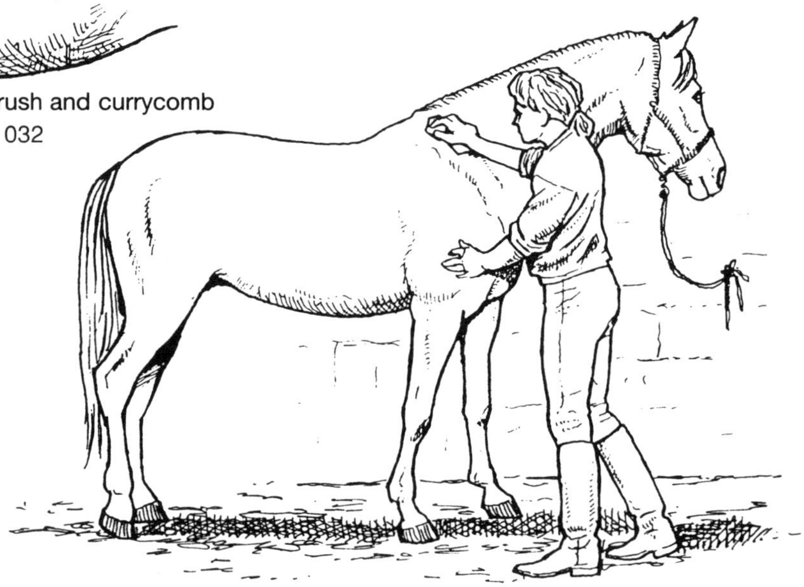

polishing coat
035

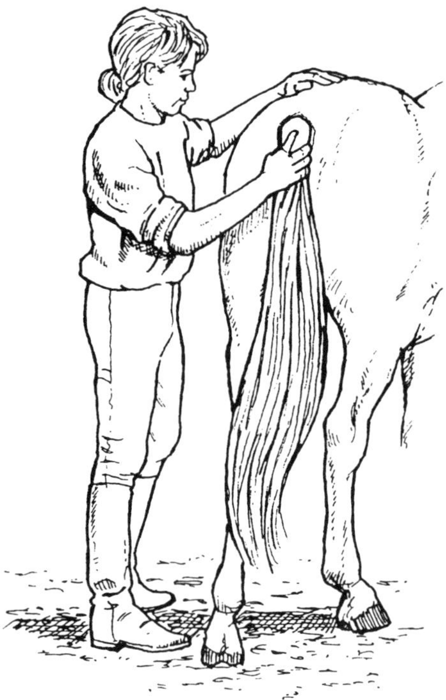

cleaning tail
034

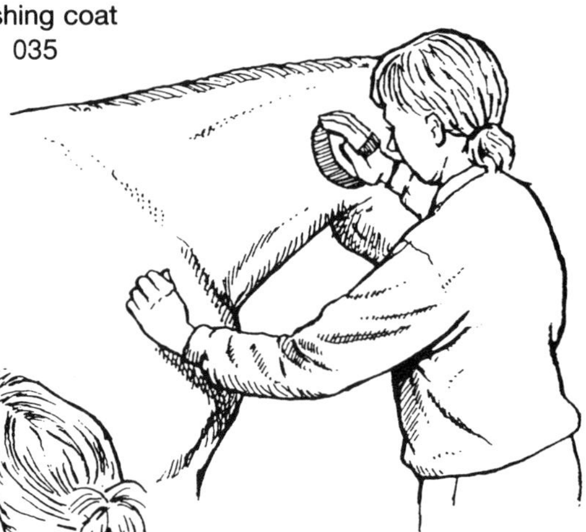

wisping
037

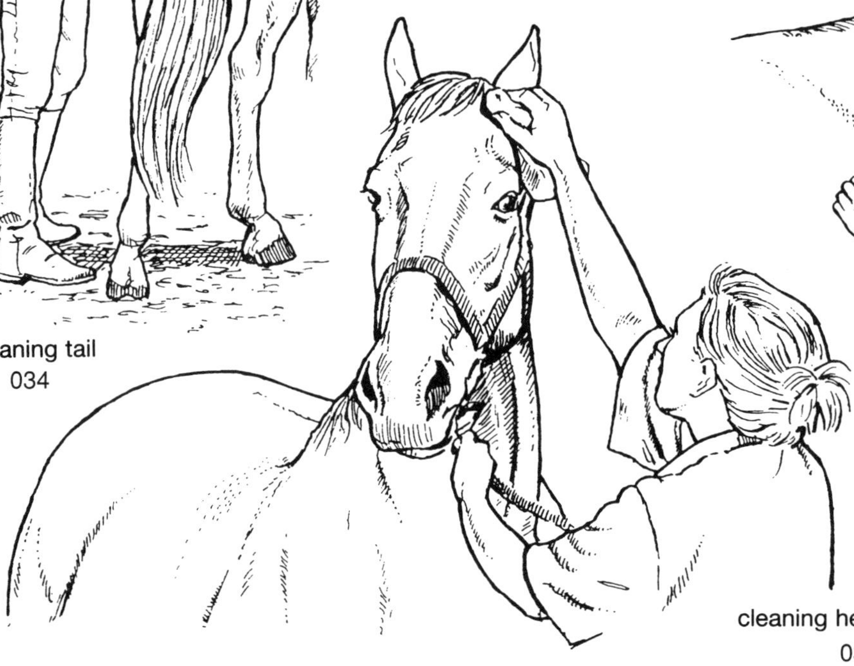

cleaning head and eyes
036

Grooming Horse—Preparing for a Show

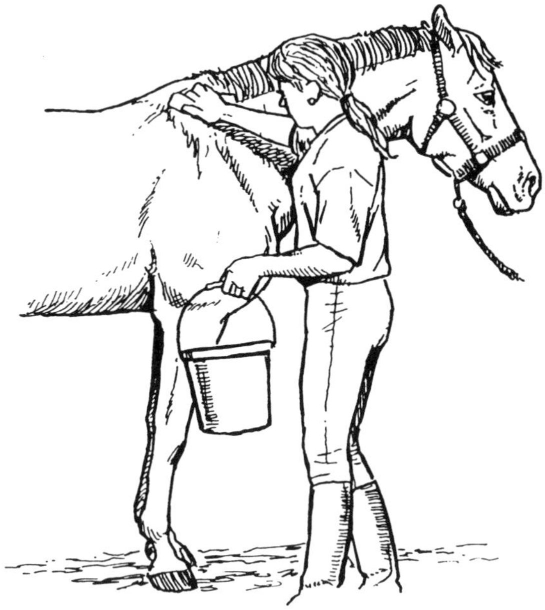

washing
038

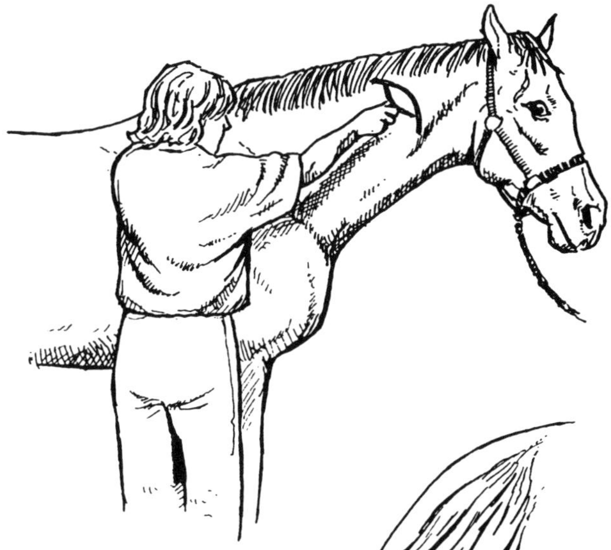

using a sweat scraper
to remove water
039

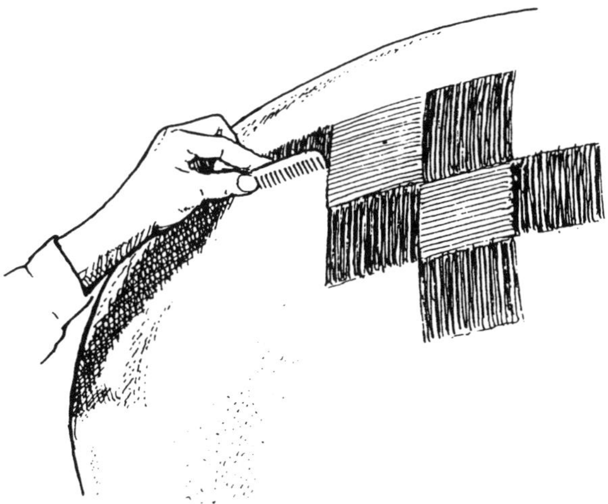

quartering marks
040

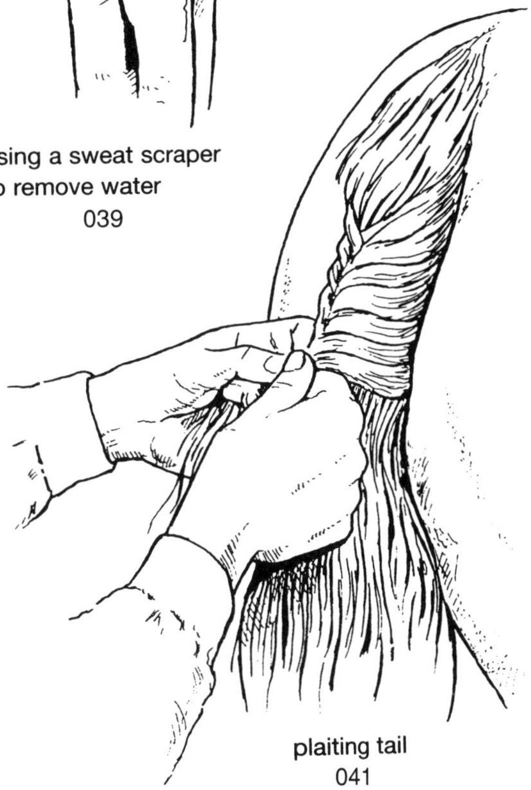

plaiting tail
041

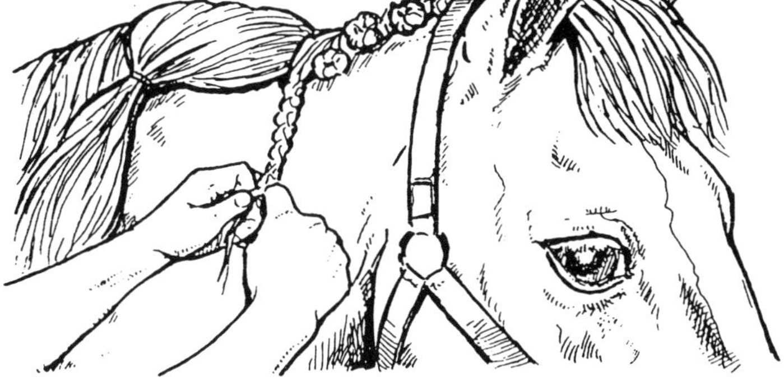

plaiting mane
042

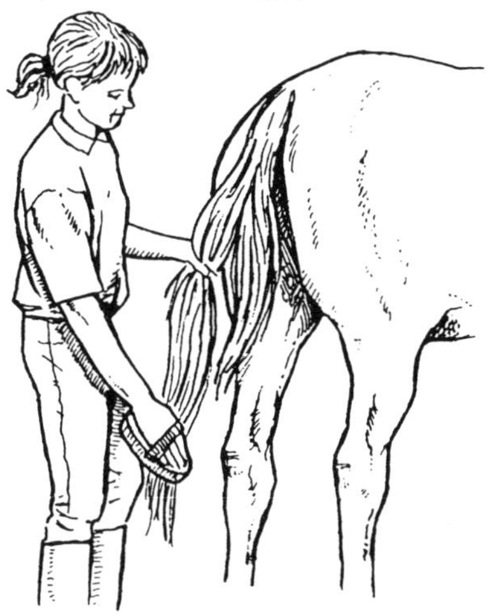

brushing out tail
043

Feeding

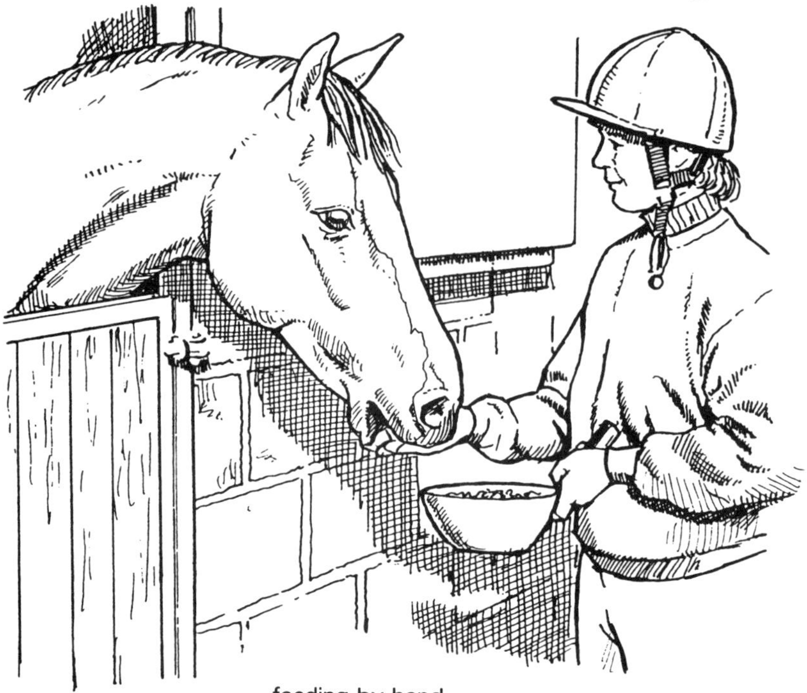

feeding by hand
044

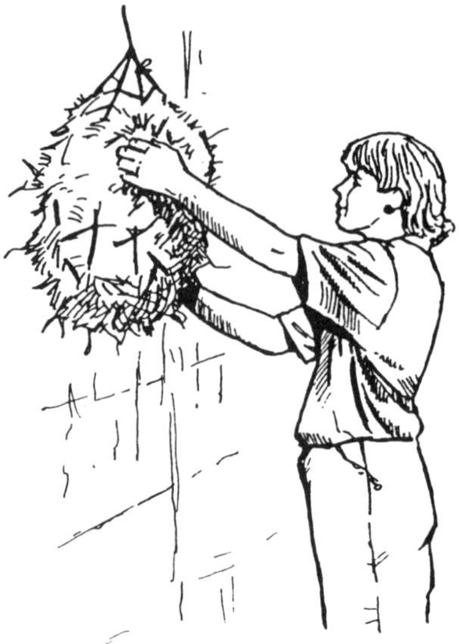

hay basket or haynet
045

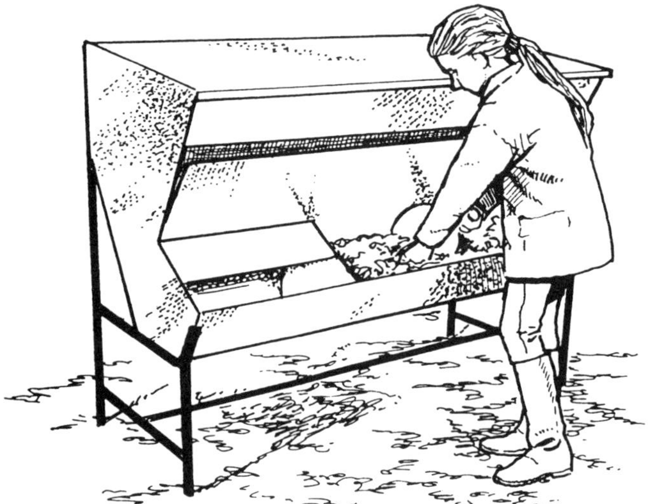

food bin, hopper bin
046

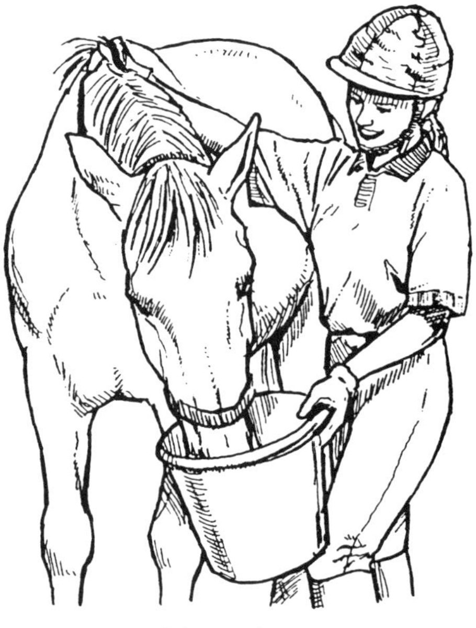

giving water
047

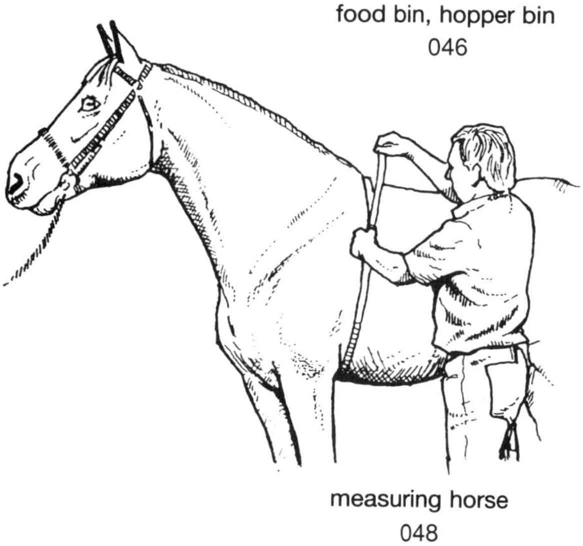

measuring horse
048

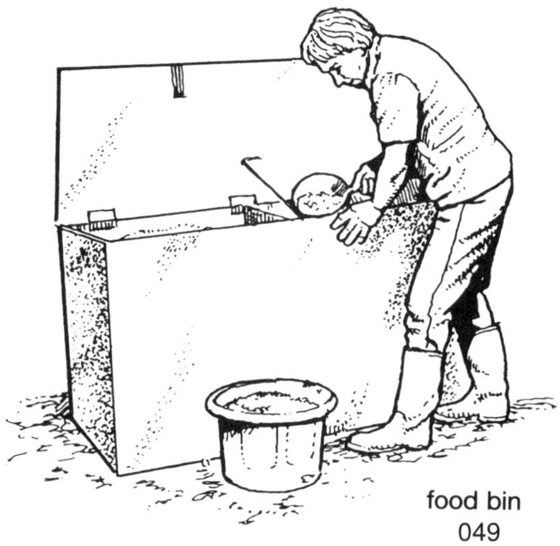

food bin
049

General Care, Mucking Out the Stable

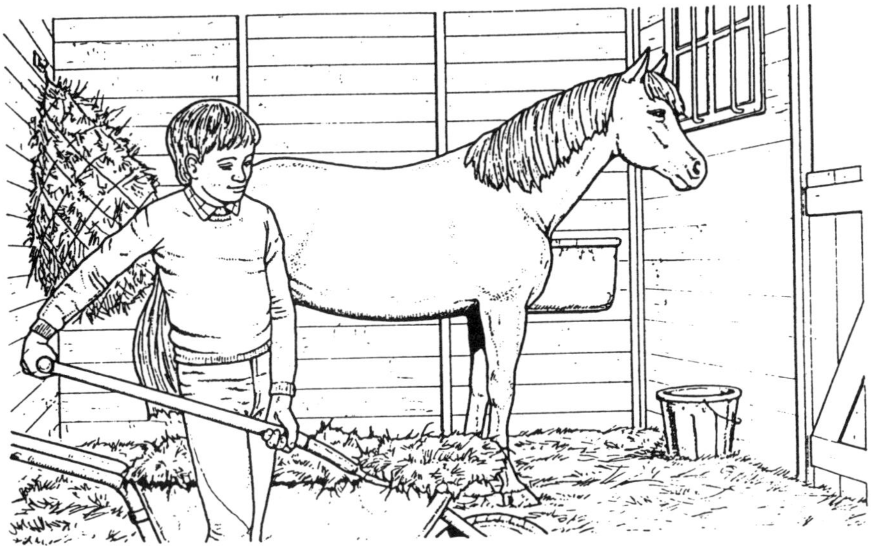

mucking out with horse in stable
050

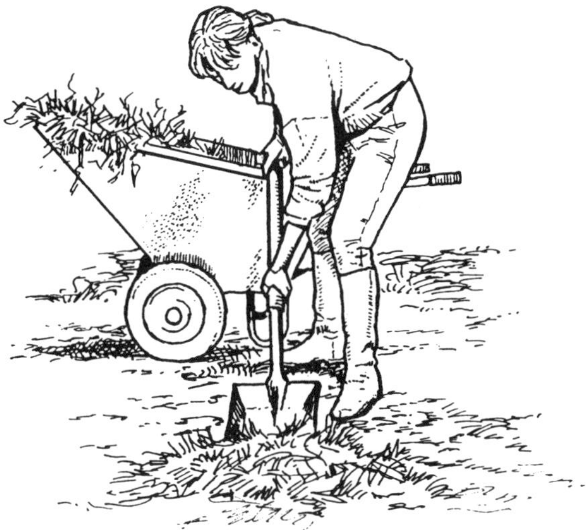

mucking out dirty bedding
051

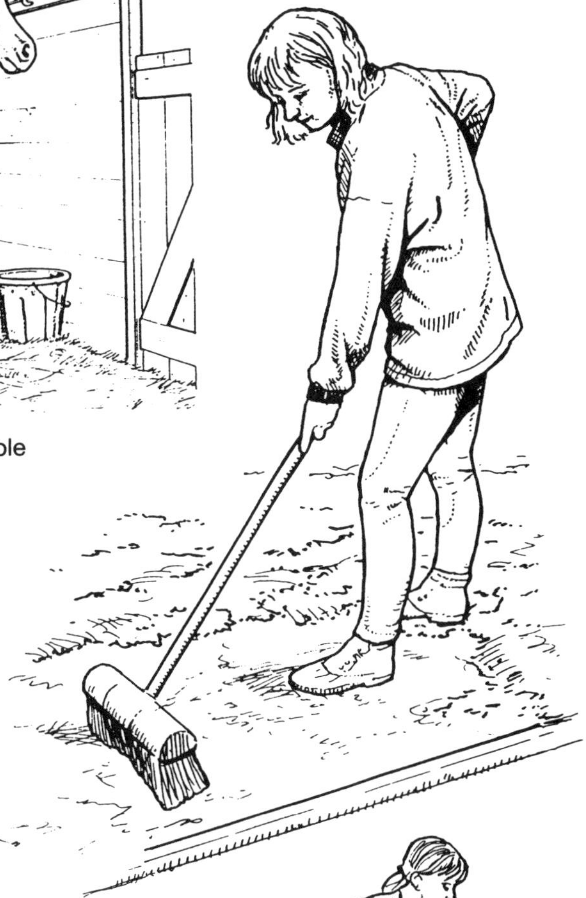

brushing stable floor
052

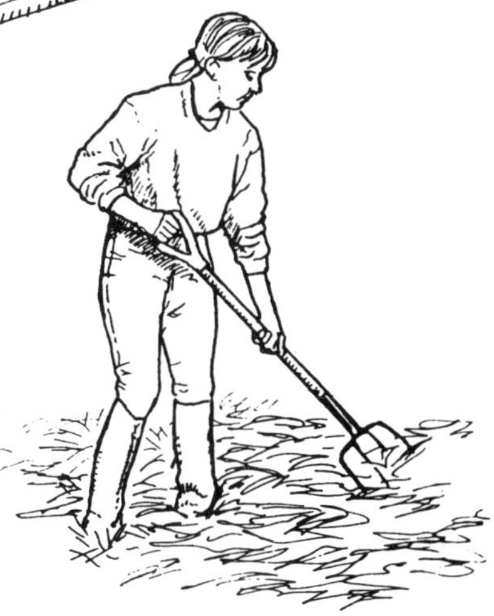

separating clean straw
053

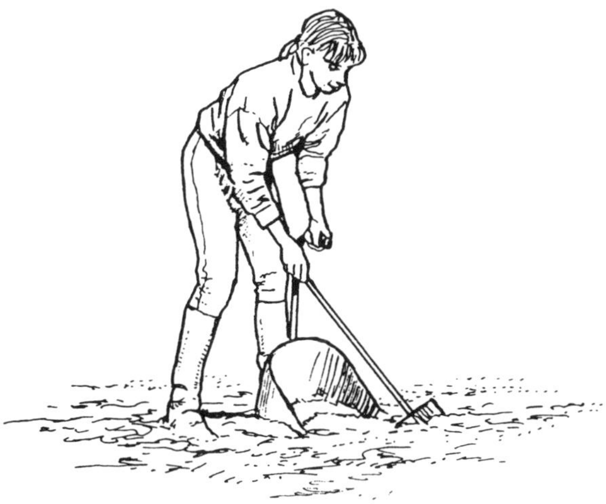

mucking out wood shavings
054

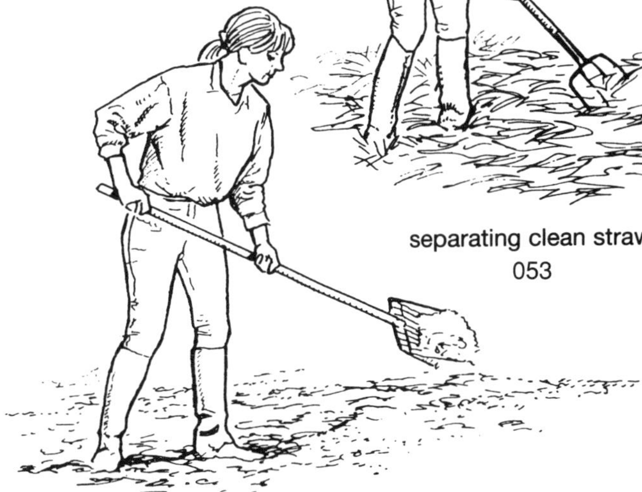

forking in clean shavings
055

Handling a Horse

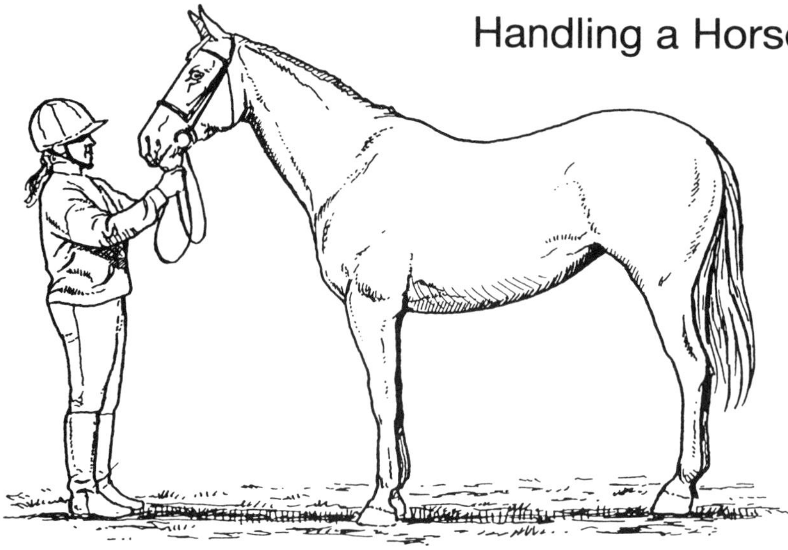

standing for inspection
056

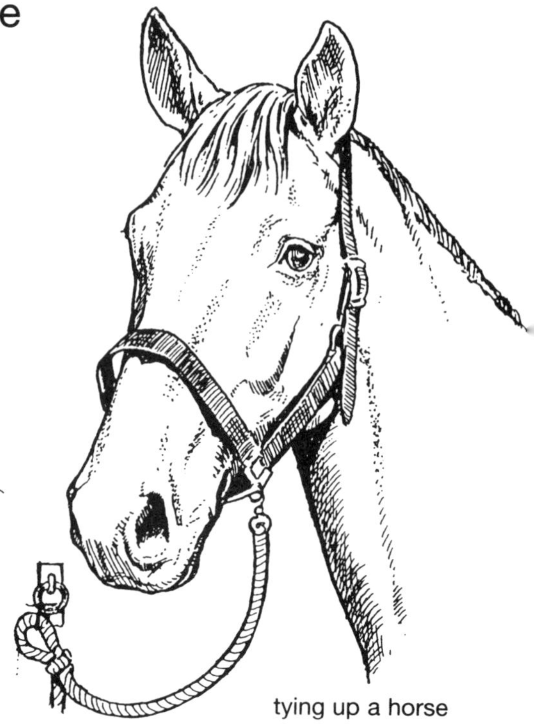

tying up a horse
057

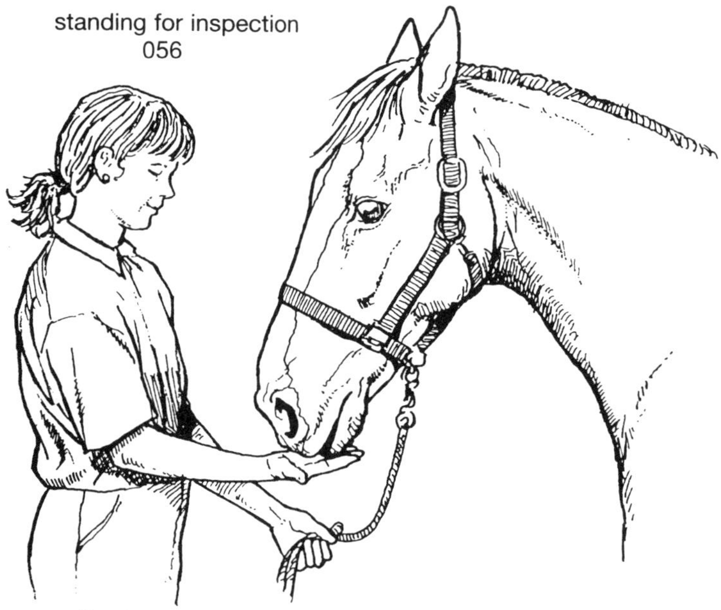

allowing the horse to smell and lick your hand 058

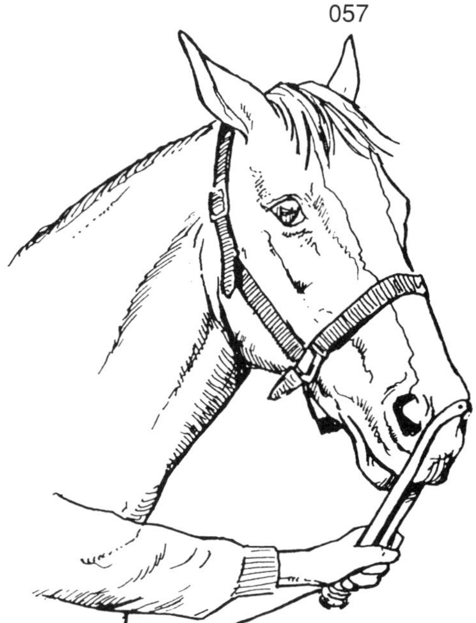

a humane twitch
059

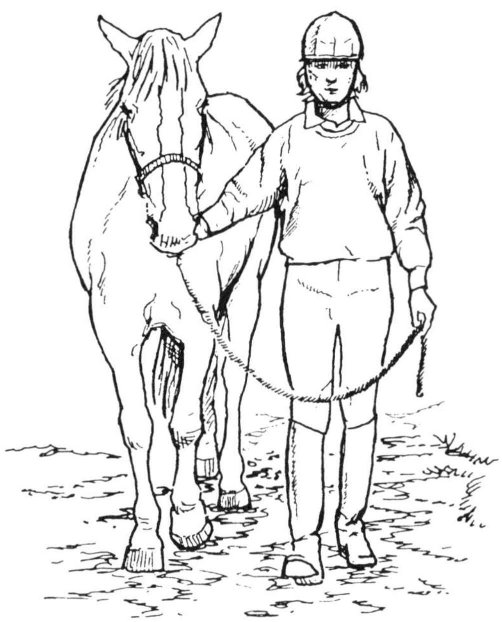

leading in a bridle
060

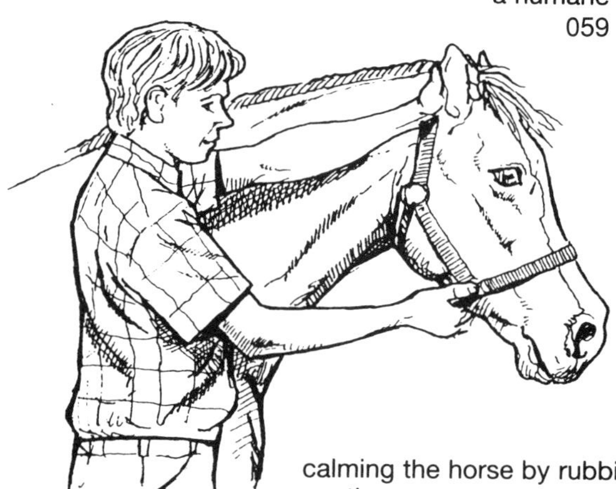

calming the horse by rubbing ears gently 061

Handling a Horse

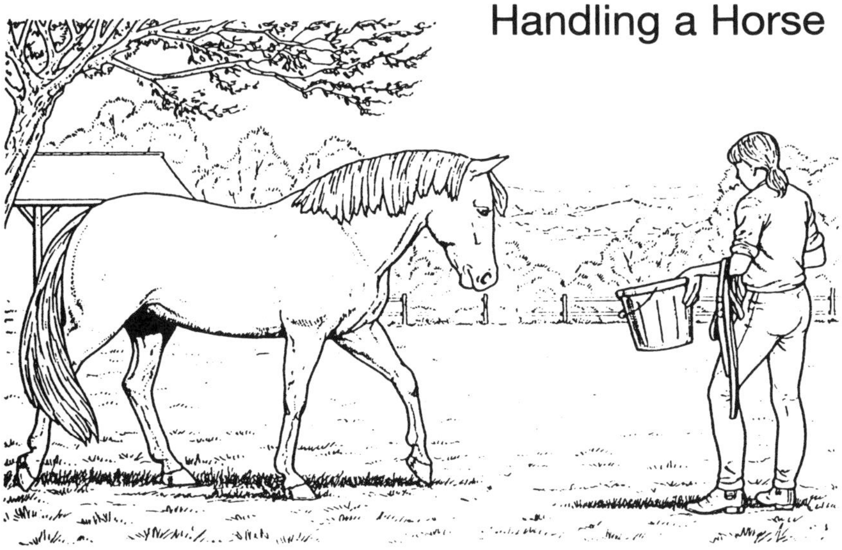

approaching horse in field
062

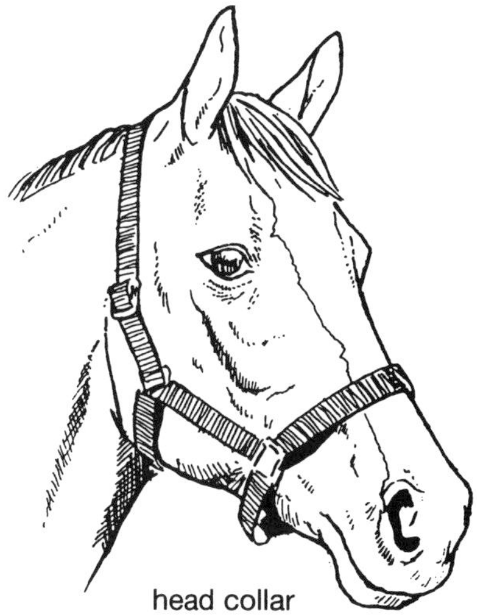

head collar
063

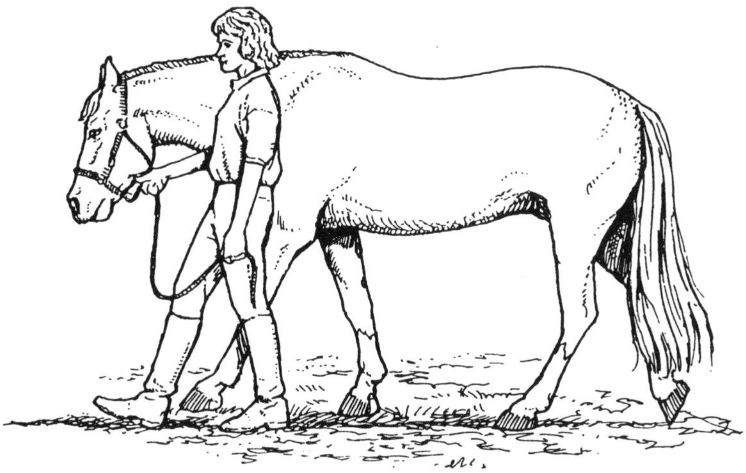

leading in a head collar
064

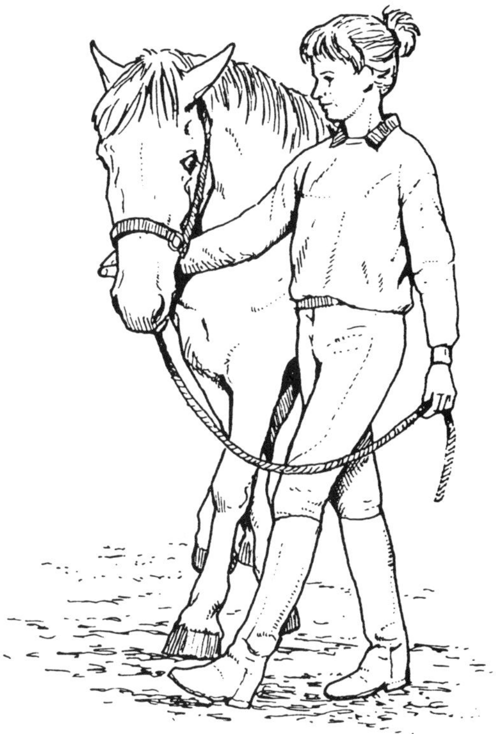

turning around
065

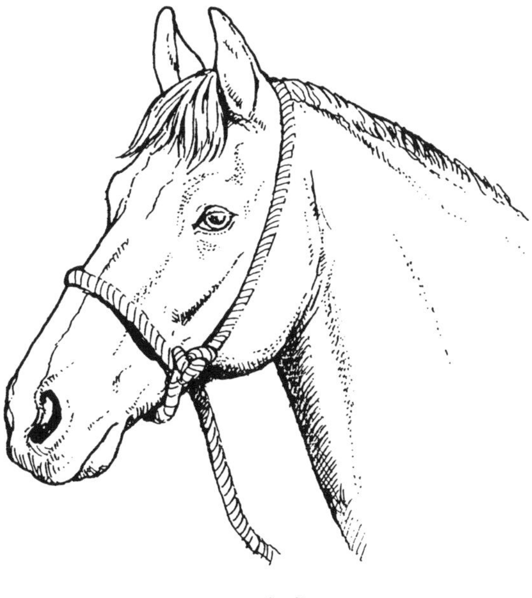

rope halter
066

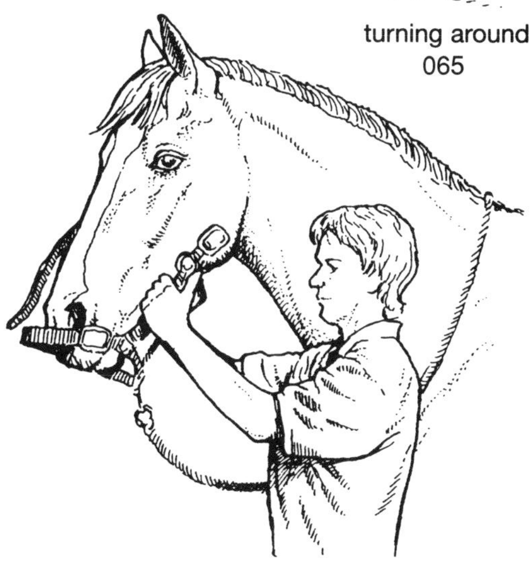

fitting head collar
067

The Stable

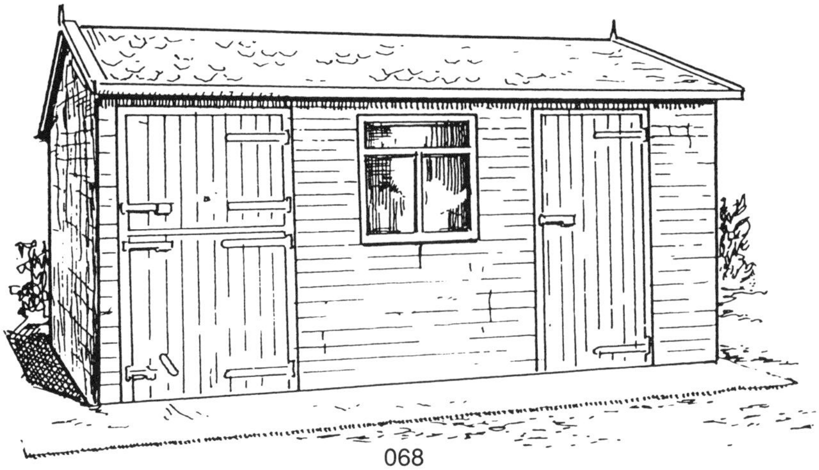

068

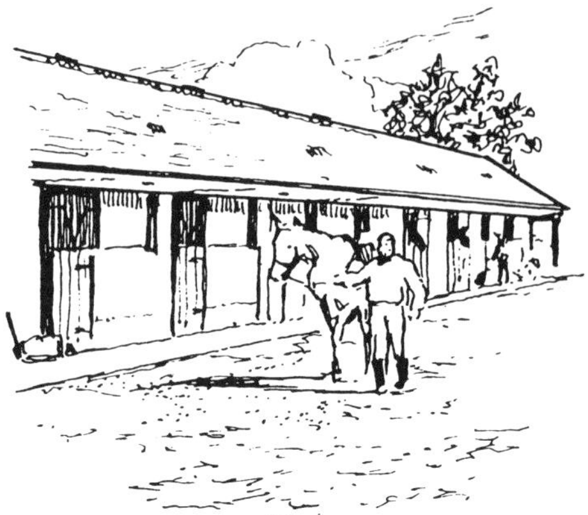

069

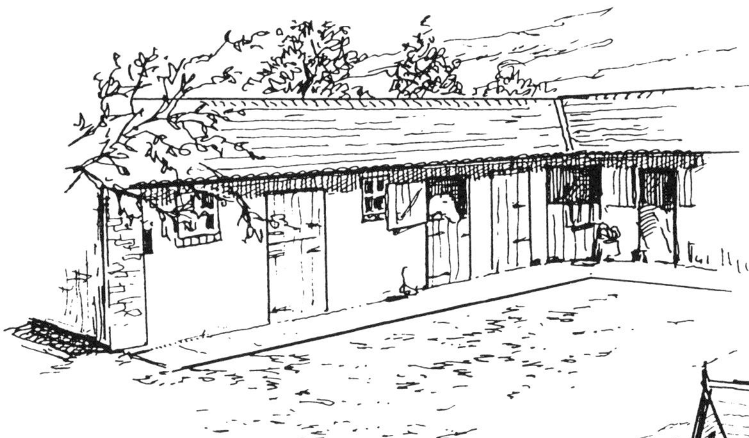

070

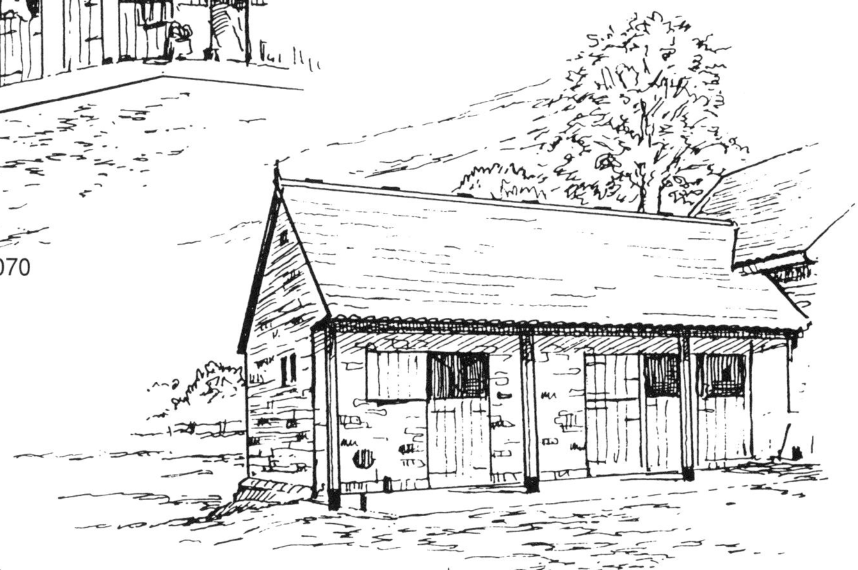

071

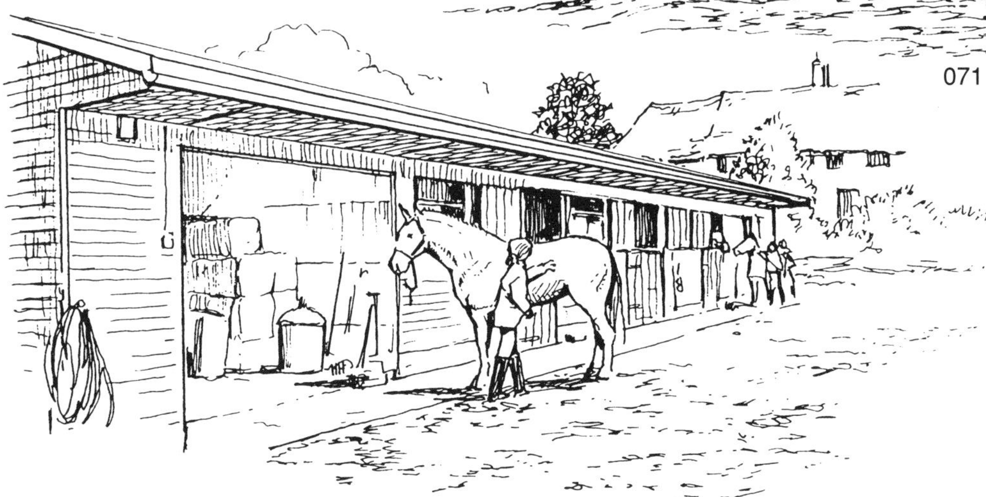

072

Horse Trailers

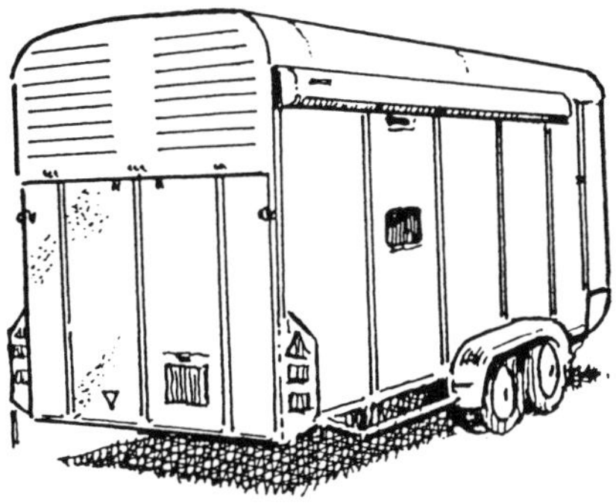

073

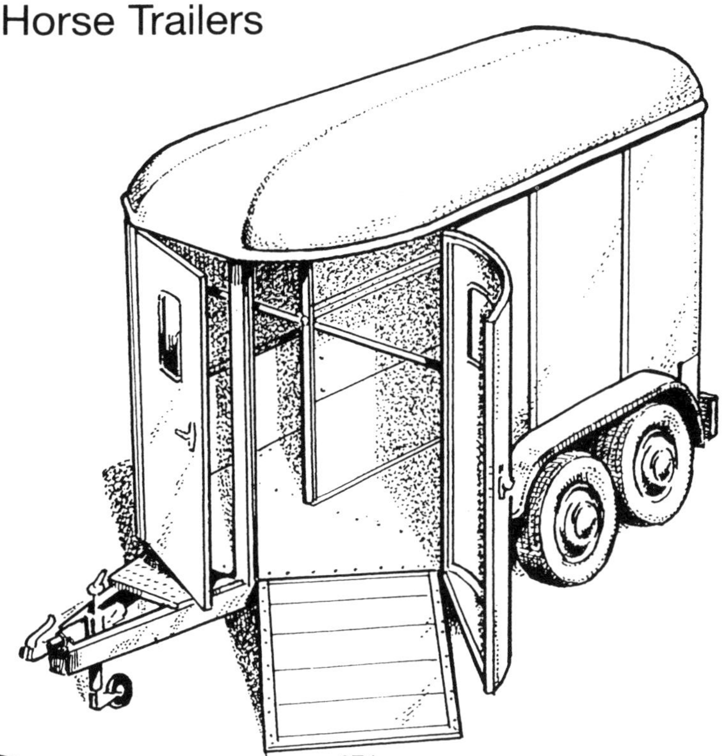

074

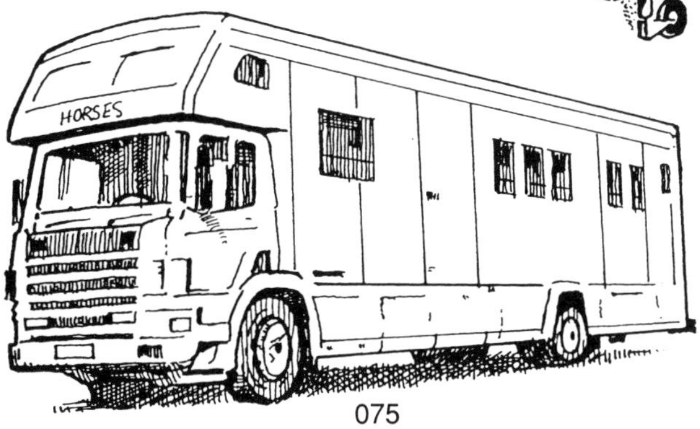

075

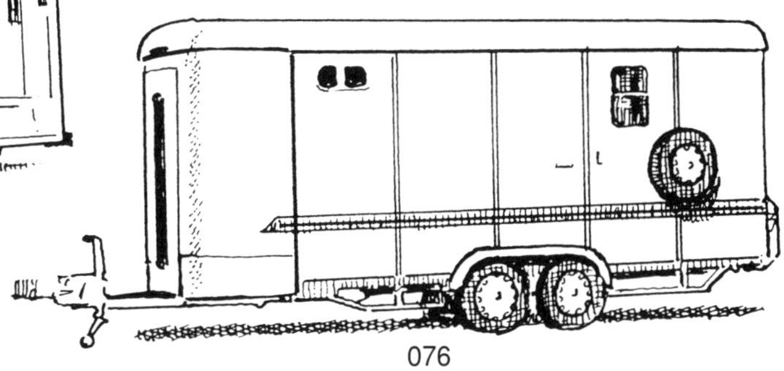

076

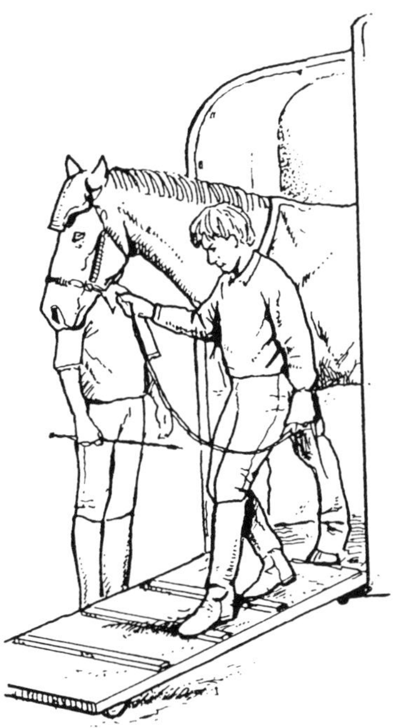

unloading the horse
077

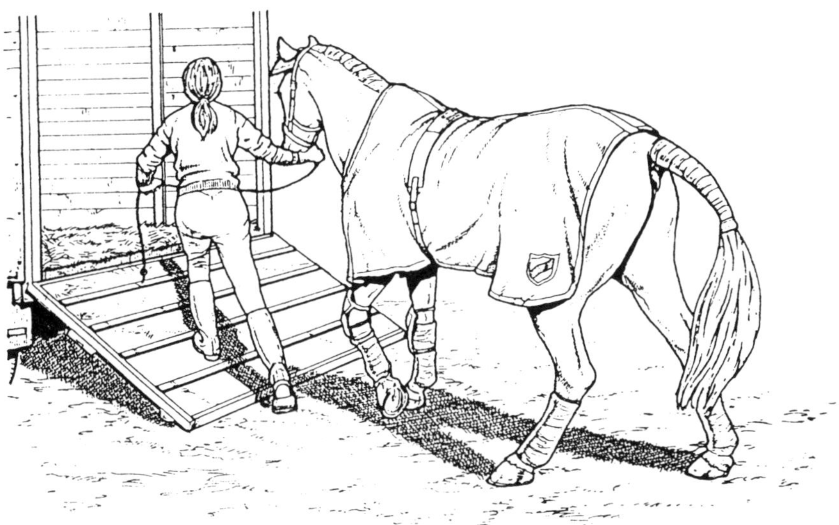

loading the horse
078

Clothing

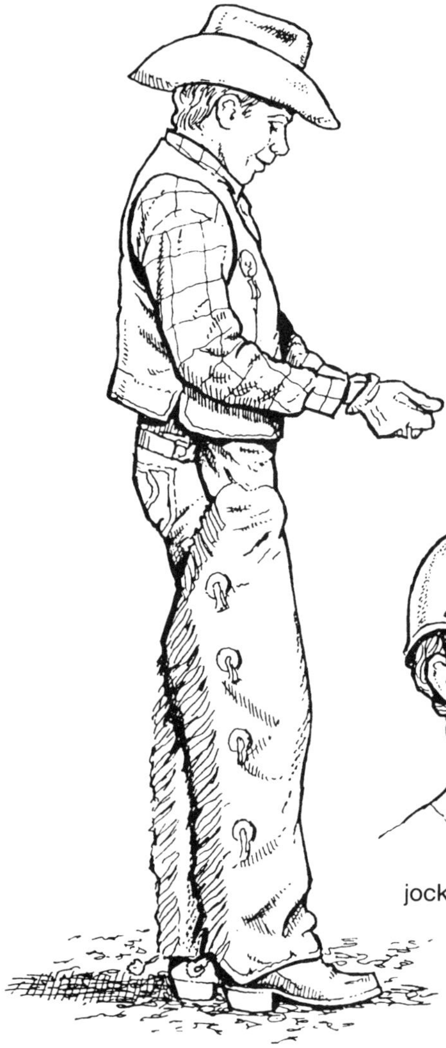

Western-style dress
079

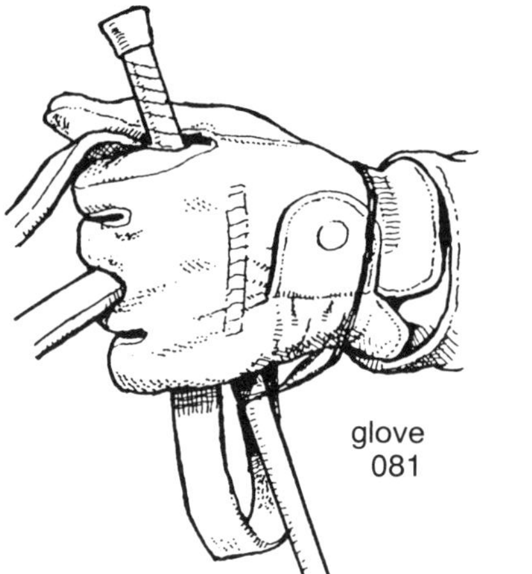

glove
081

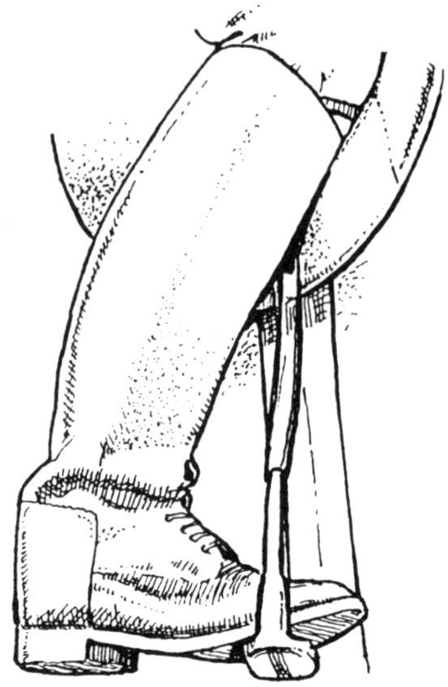

riding boot
082

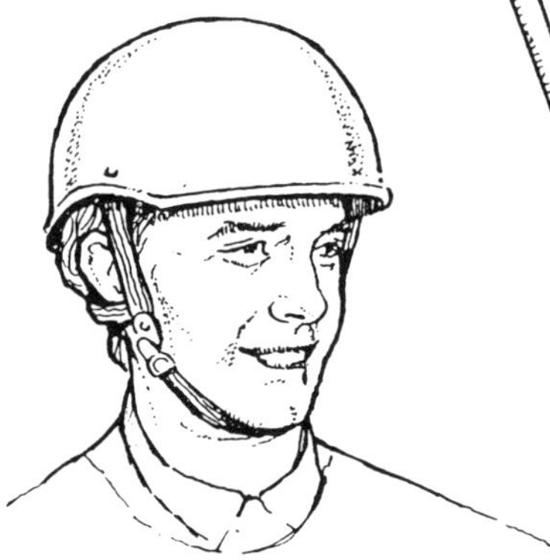

jockey skull helmet
080

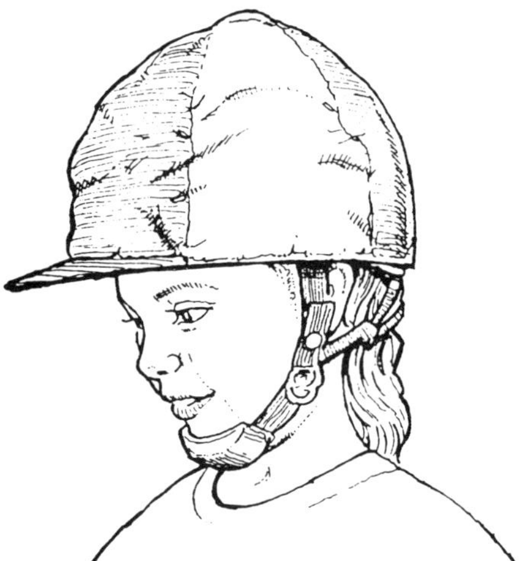

jockey skull helmet with silk cover
083

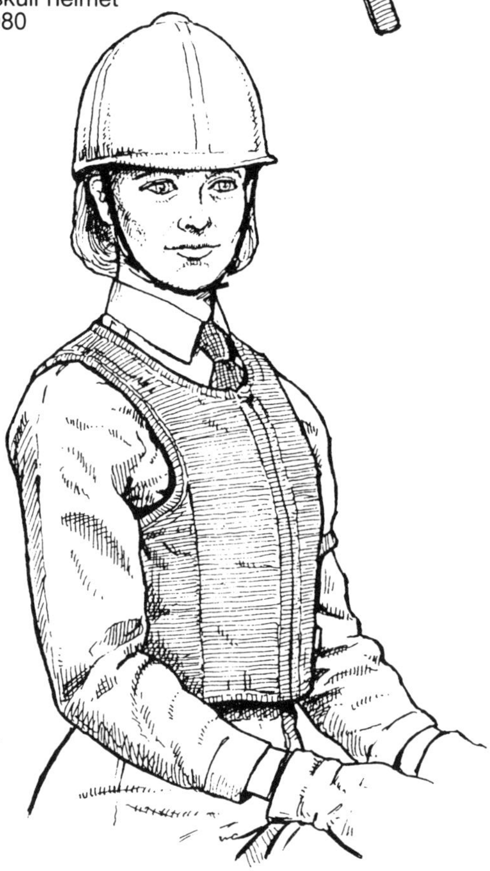

body protector
084

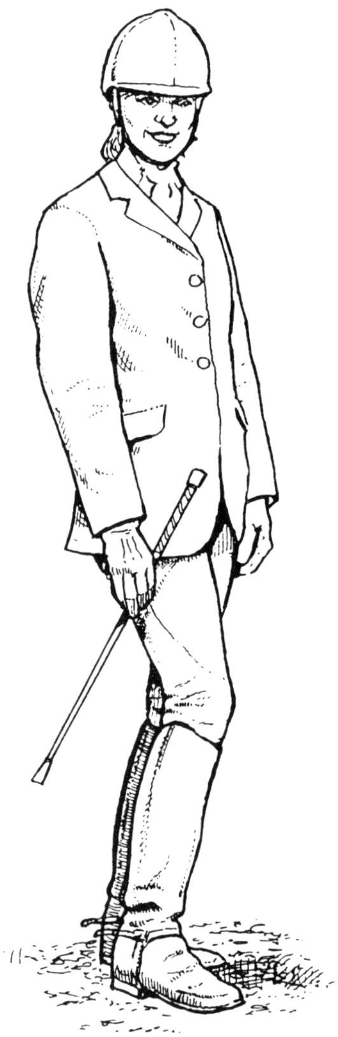

English-style dress
085

Exercises for the Rider

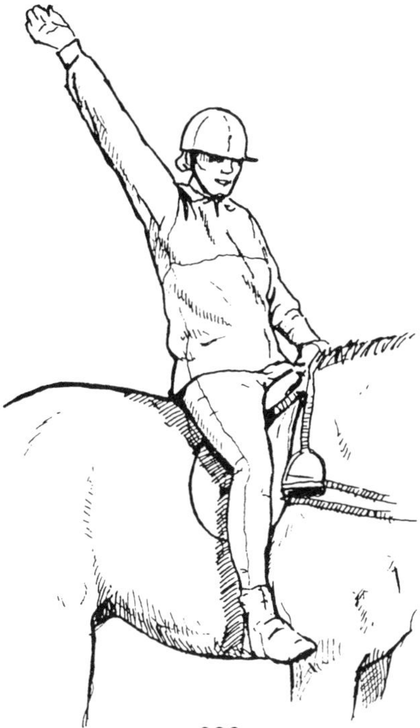

086

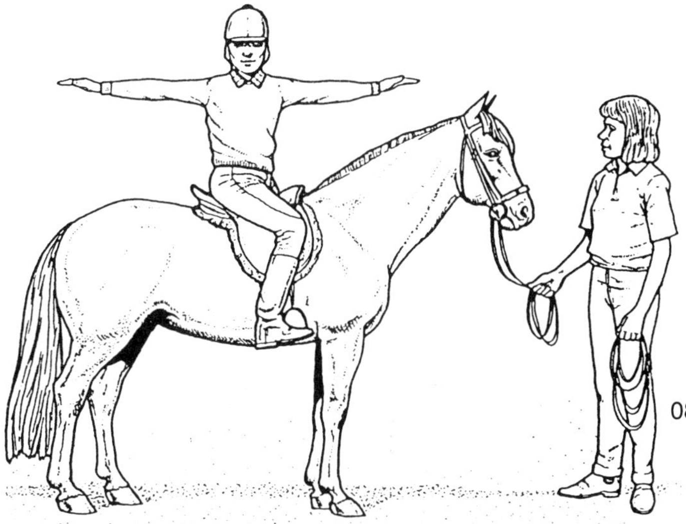

087

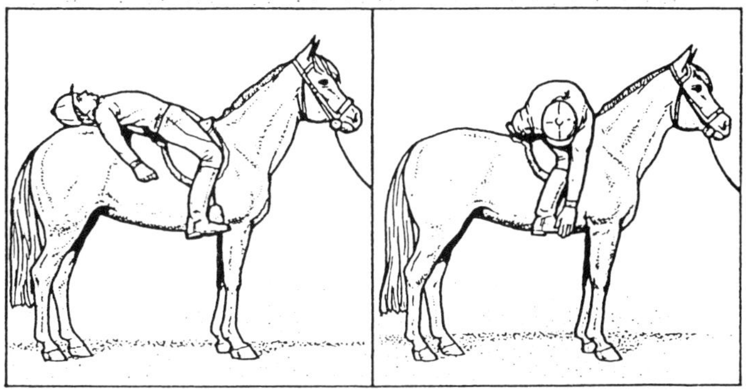

088

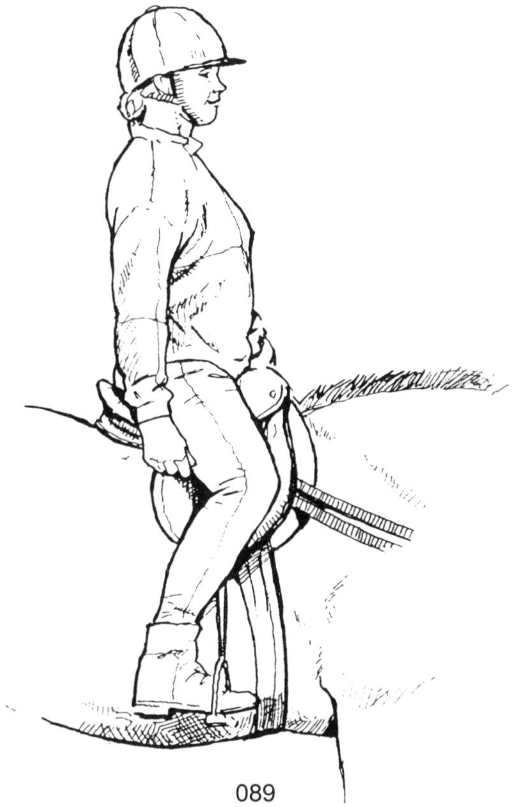

089

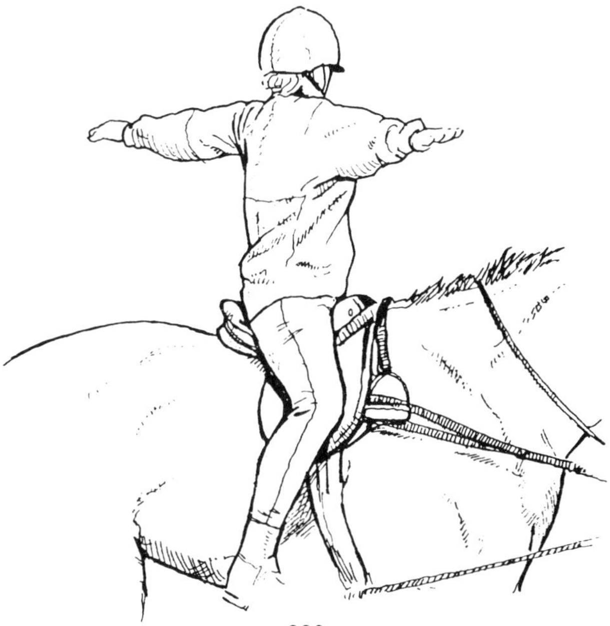

090

In the Saddle

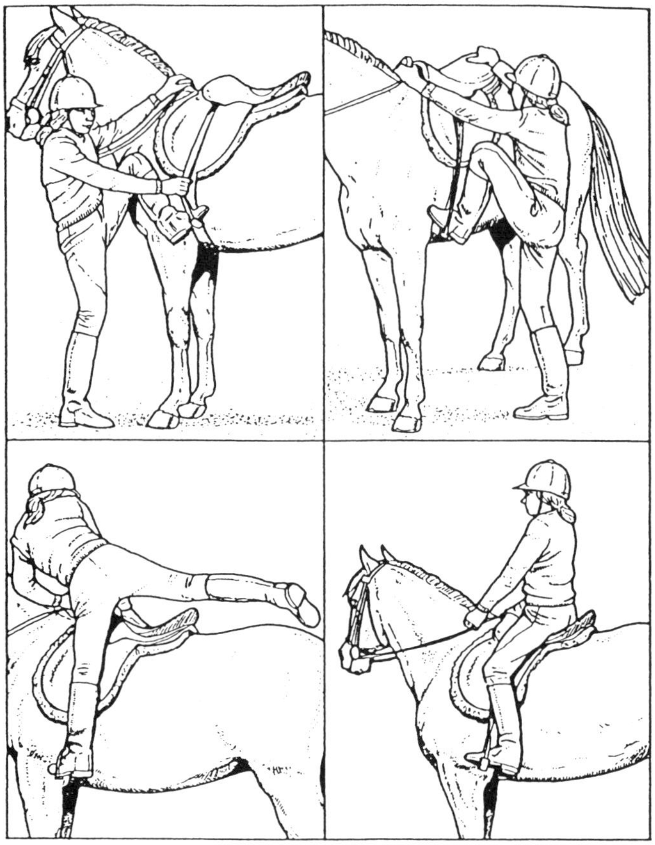

091

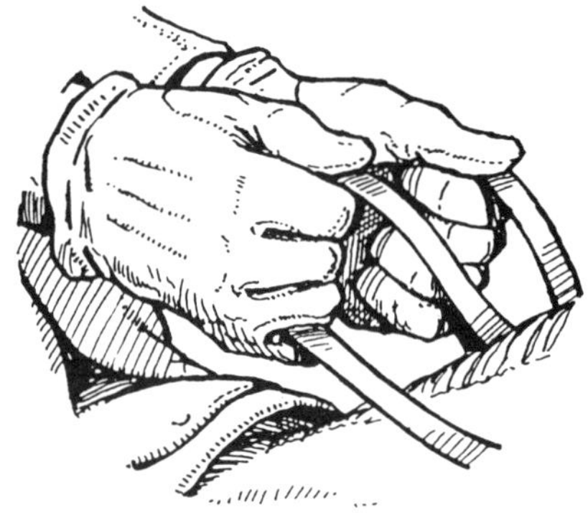

holding reins, English style
092

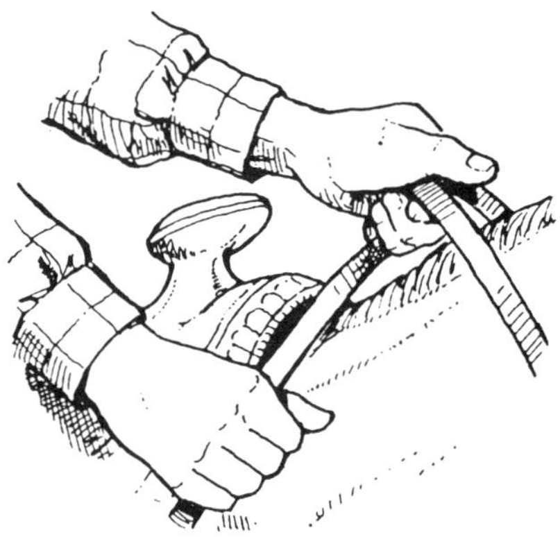

Western style
093

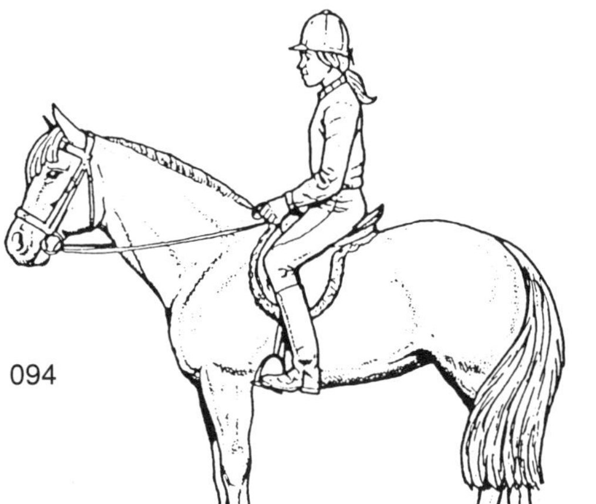

094

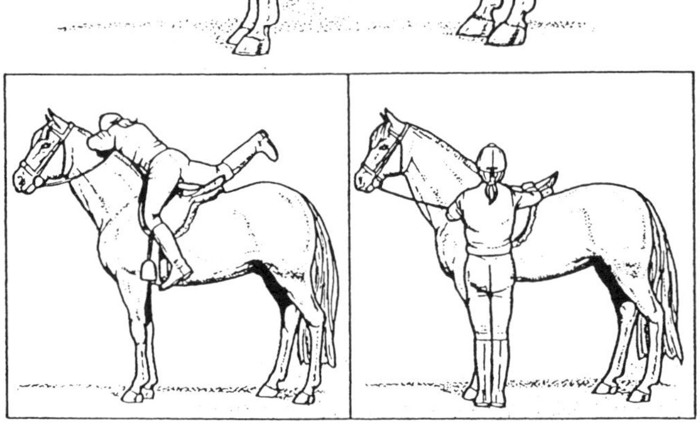

mounting and dismounting the horse
095

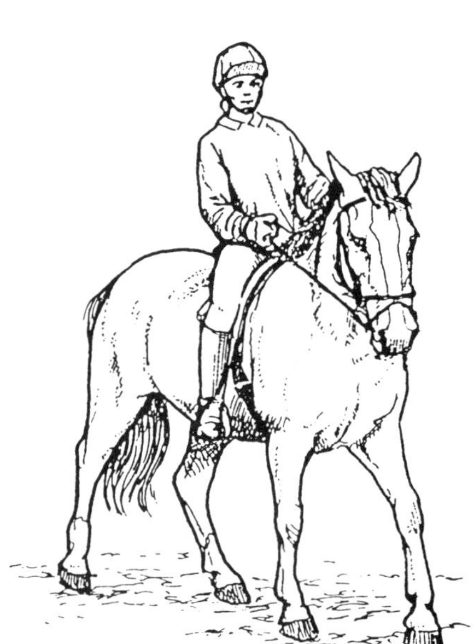

turning right
096

In the Saddle

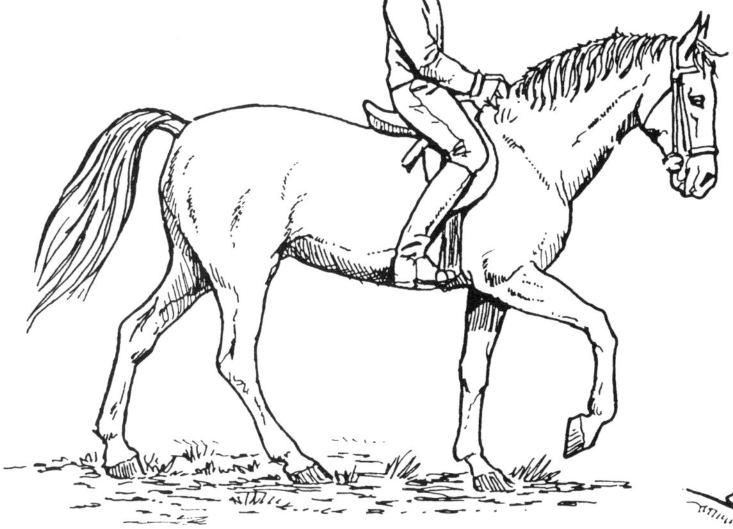

trot
097

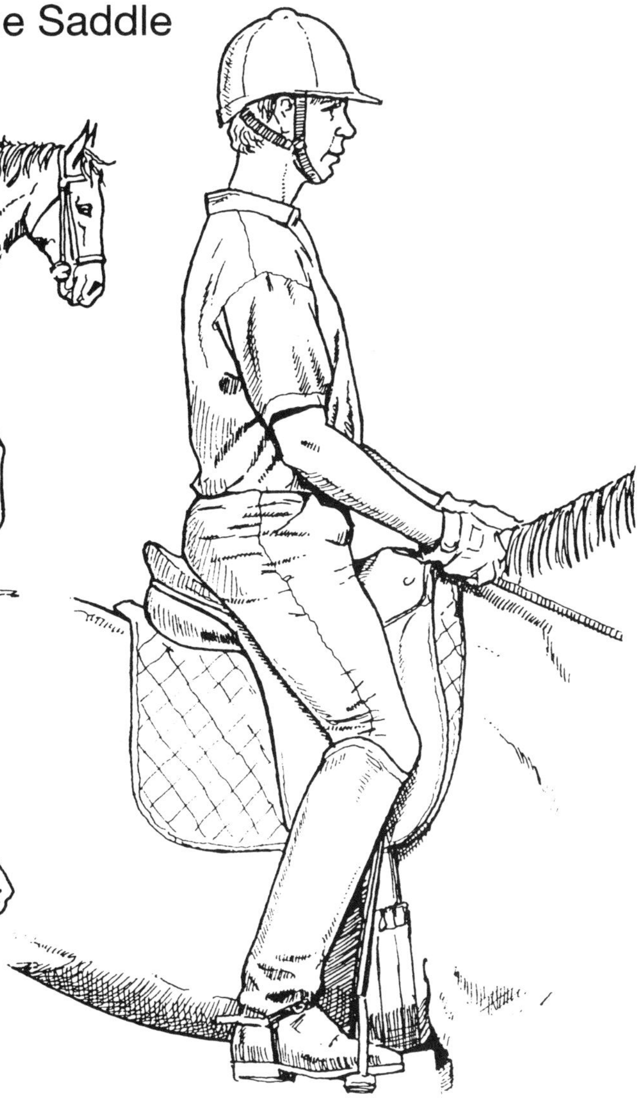

correct seat
099

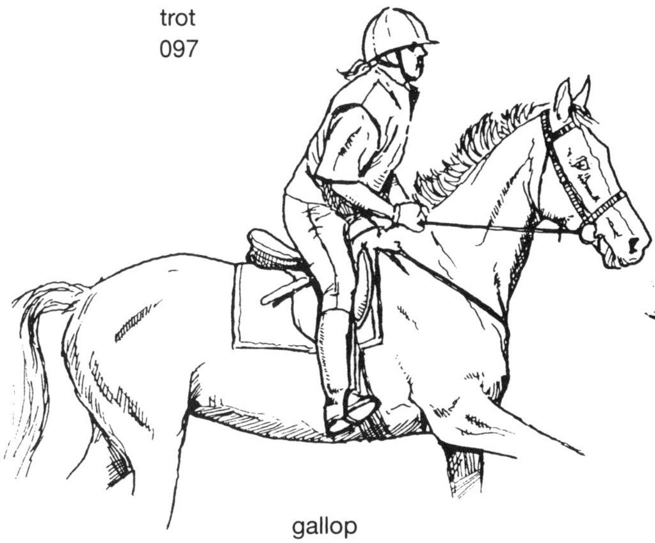

gallop
098

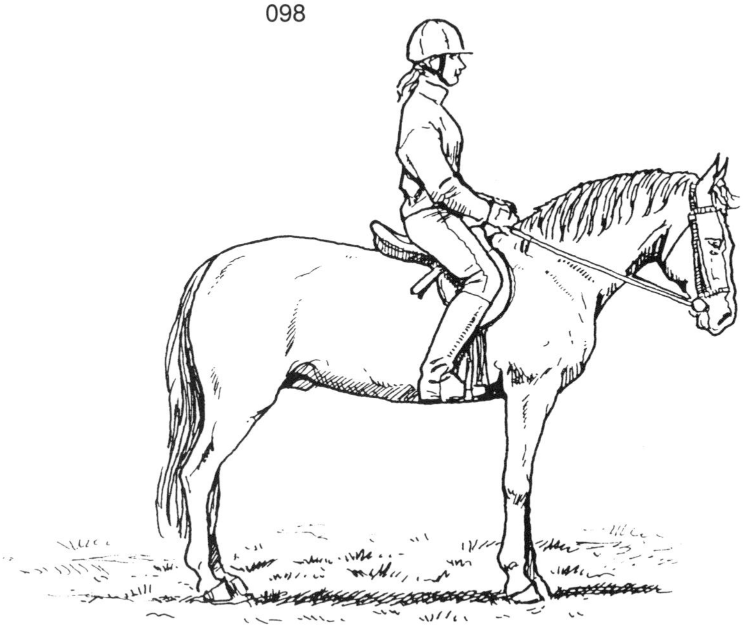

halt
100

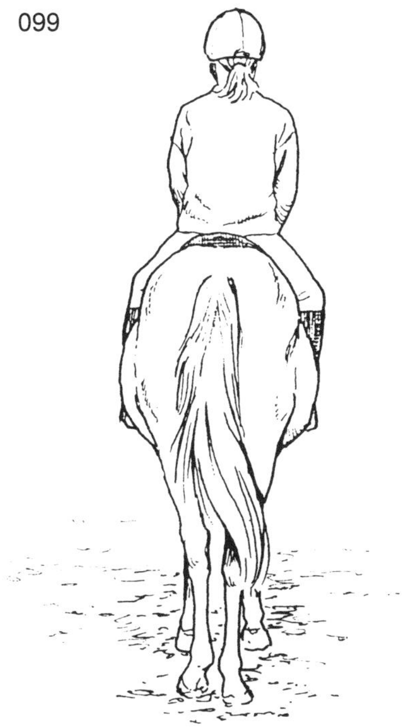

correct seat
101

Schooling Aids

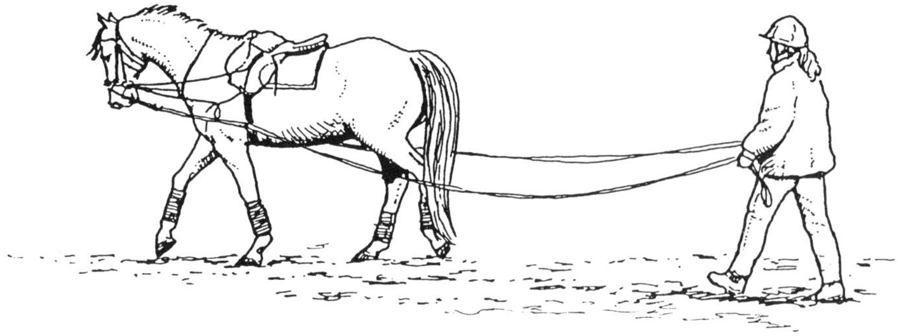

breaking in aid
102

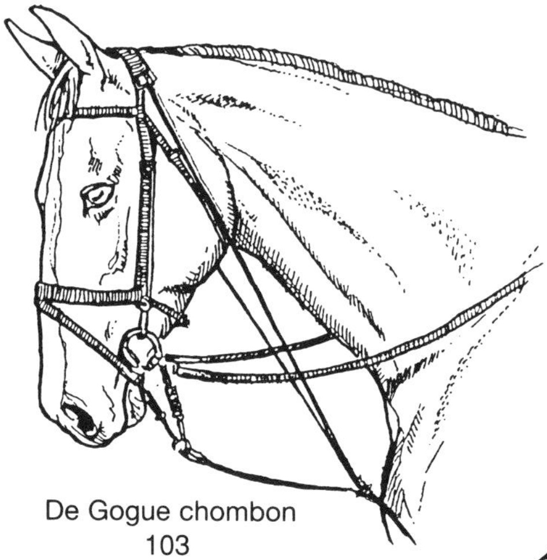

De Gogue chombon
103

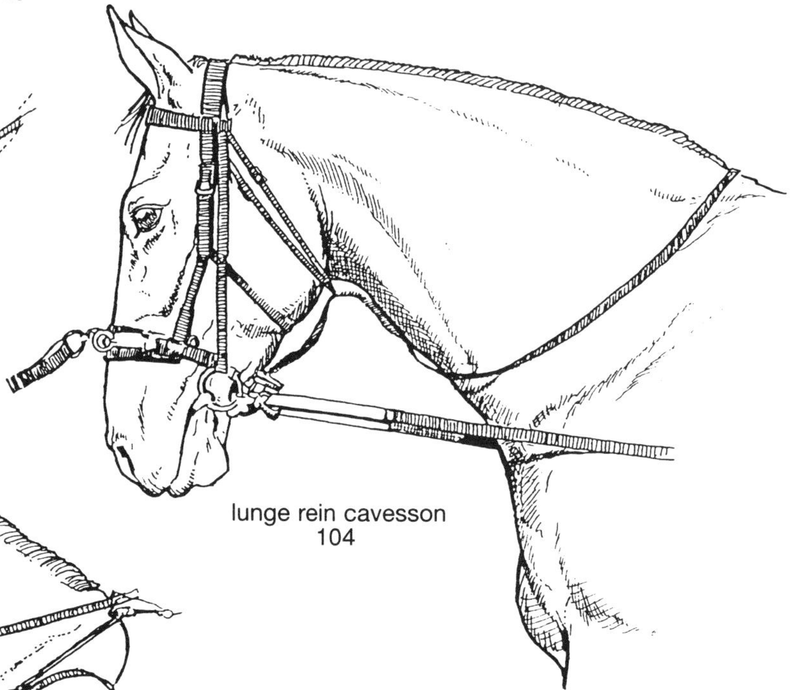

lunge rein cavesson
104

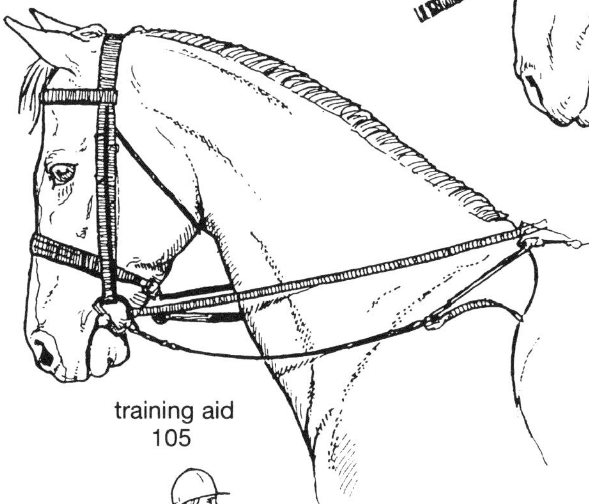

training aid
105

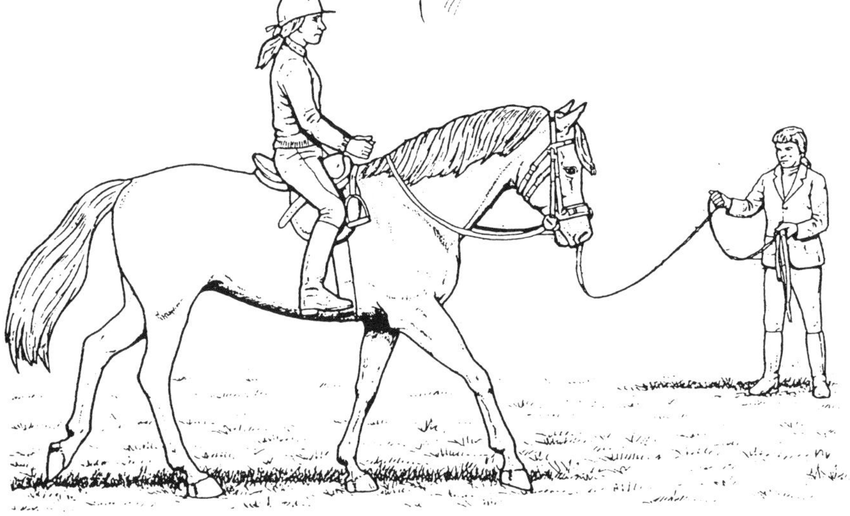

lunge rein in use
106

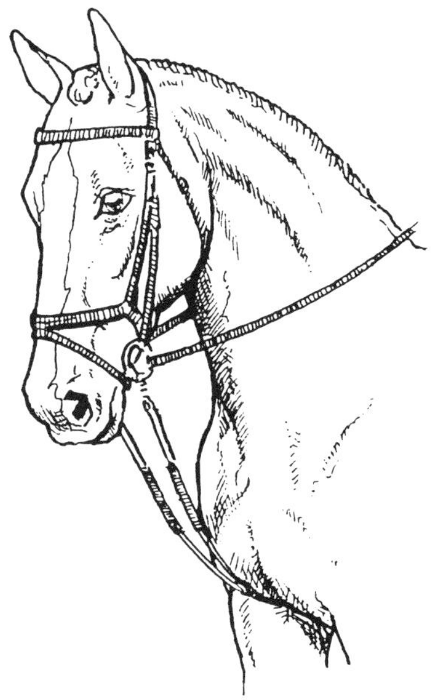

Harbridge training aid (Martingale)
107

Learning to Jump

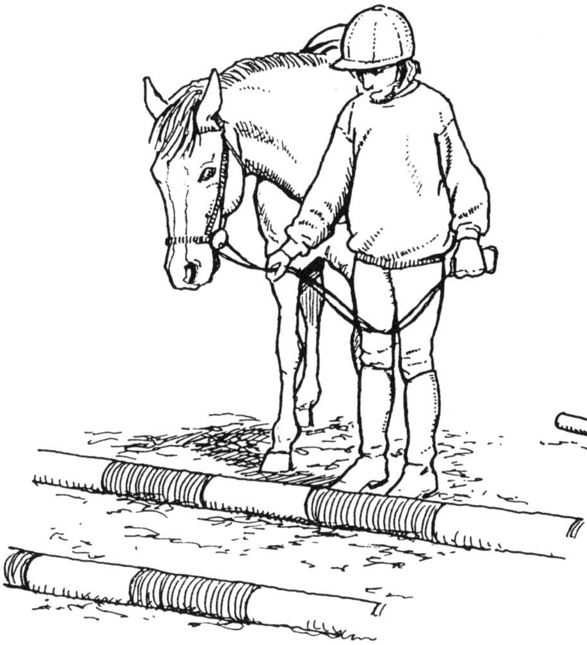

allowing horse to see the poles
108

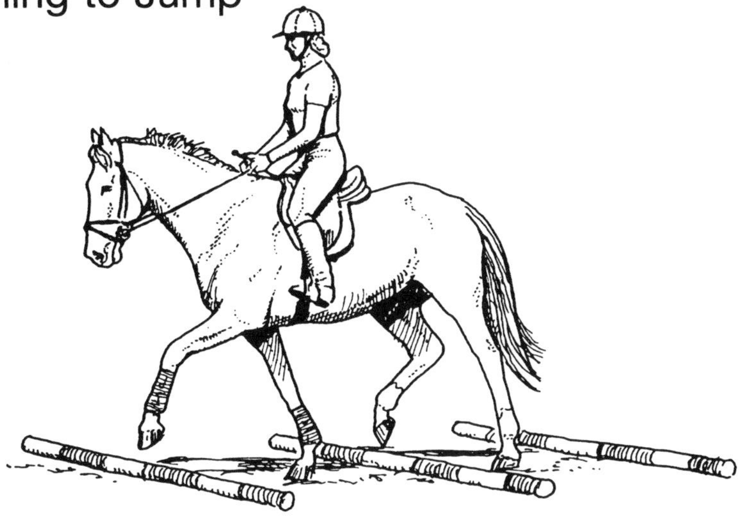

walking over poles
109

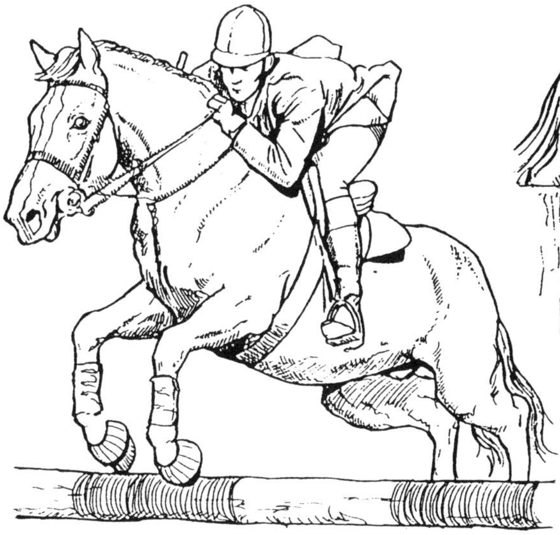

a good jump
110

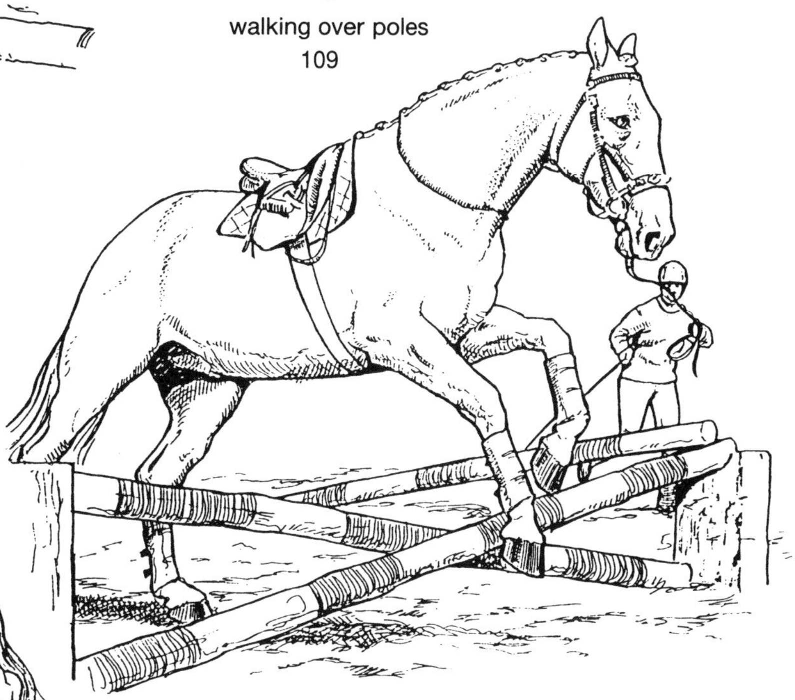

jumping with lunge rein
111

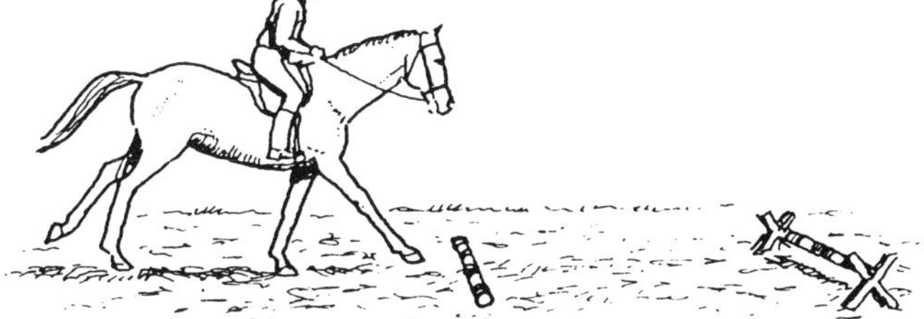

pacing a horse to jump
112

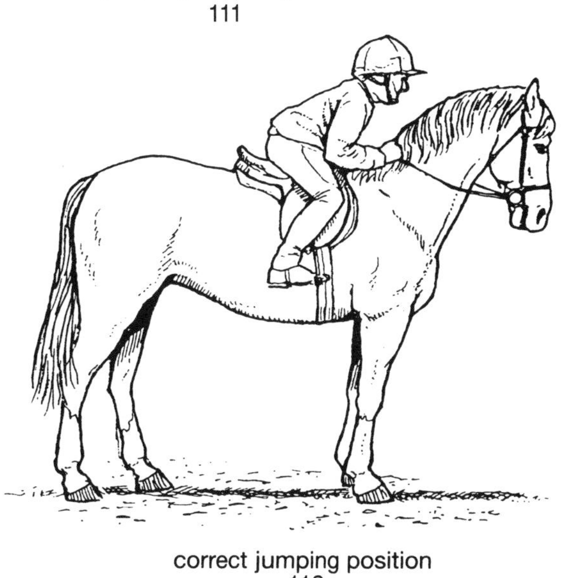

correct jumping position
113

Saddles

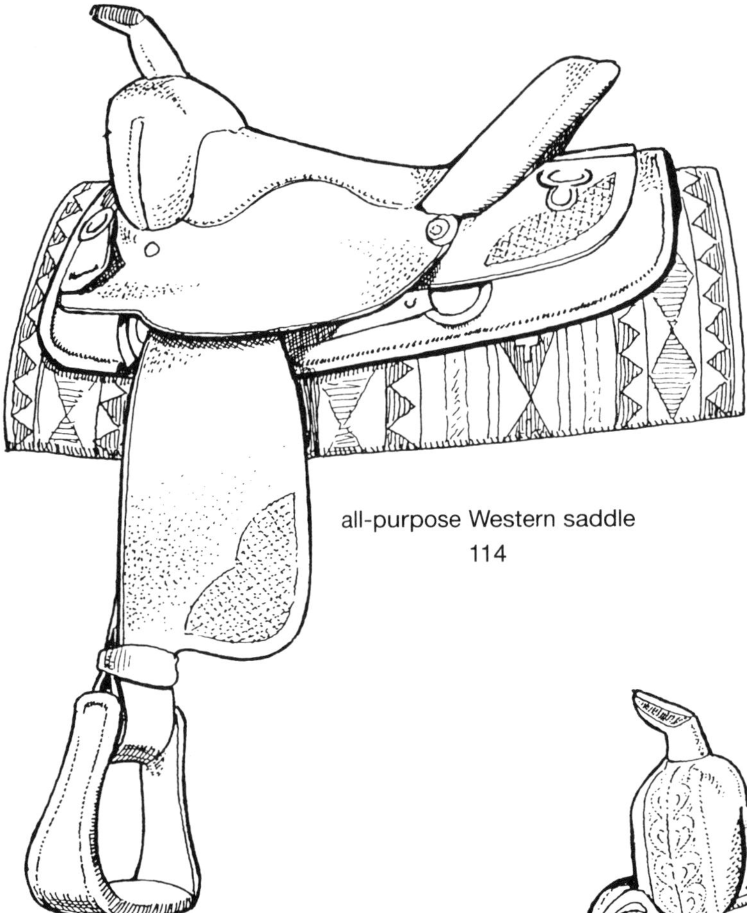

all-purpose Western saddle
114

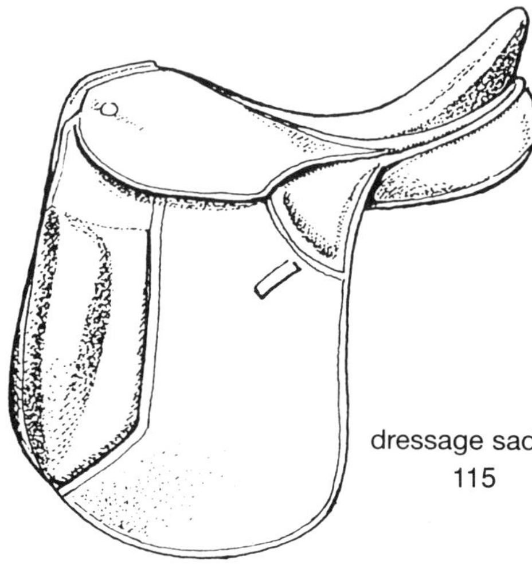

dressage saddle
115

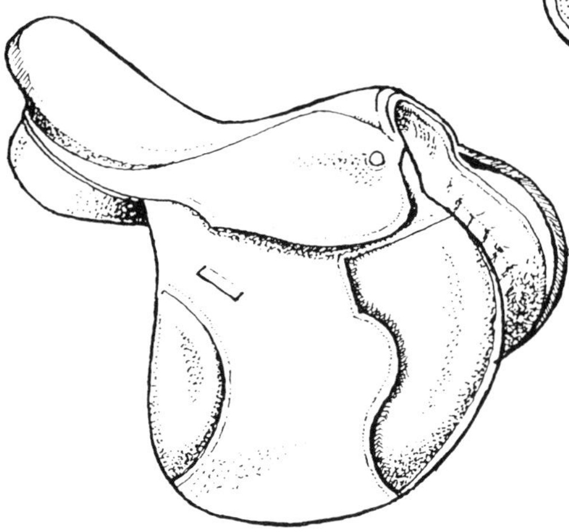

jumping saddle
116

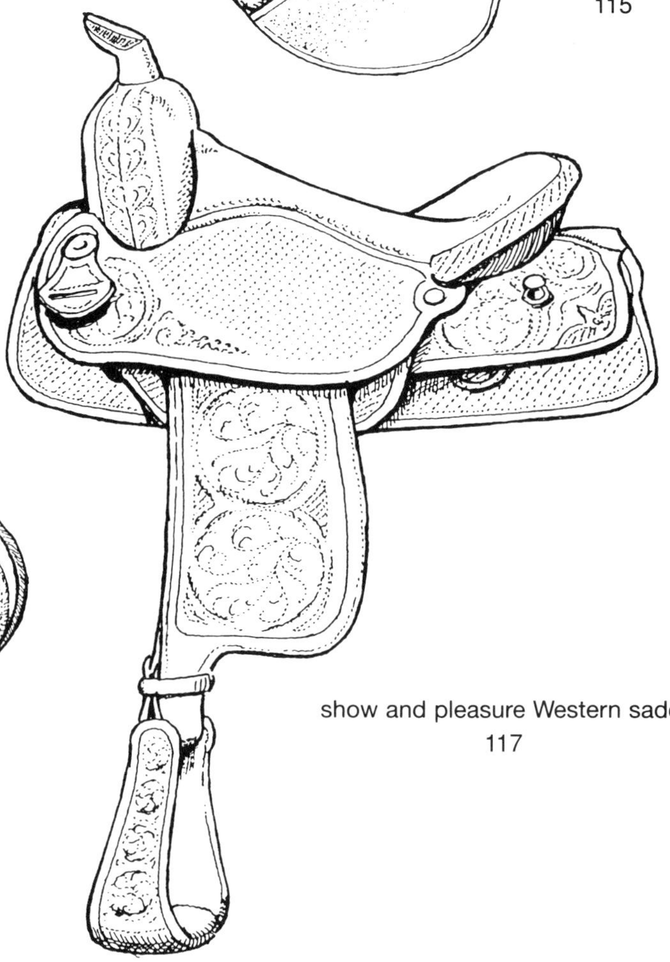

show and pleasure Western saddle
117

Saddles

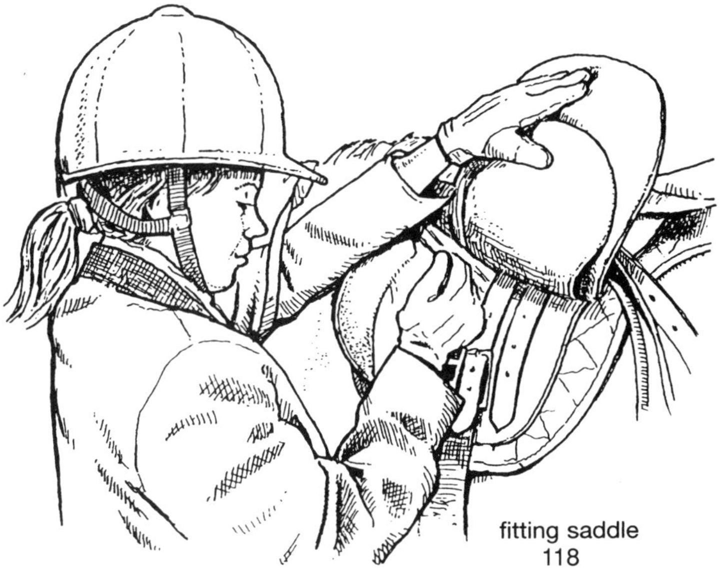

fitting saddle
118

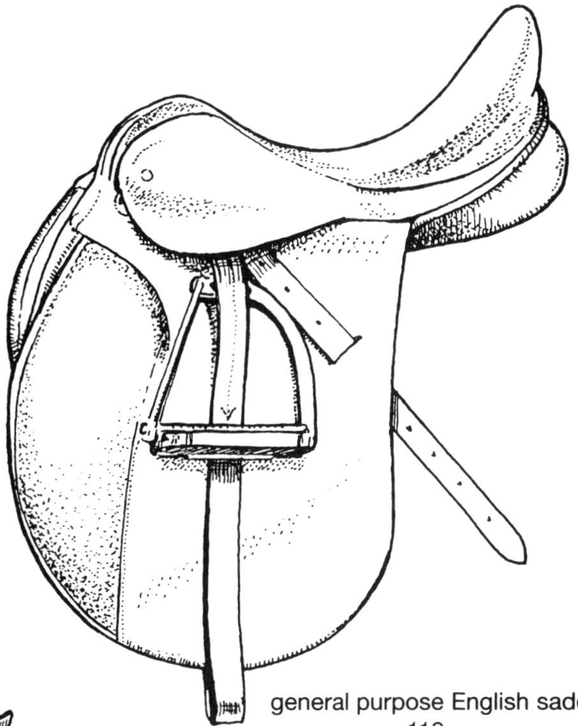

general purpose English saddle
119

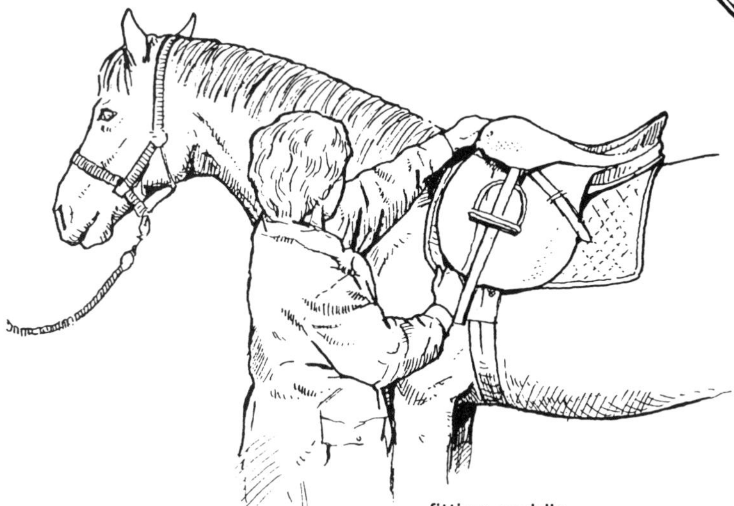

fitting saddle
120

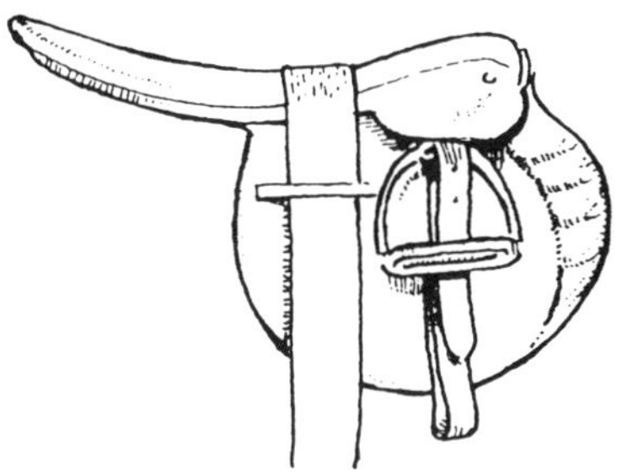

racing saddle
121

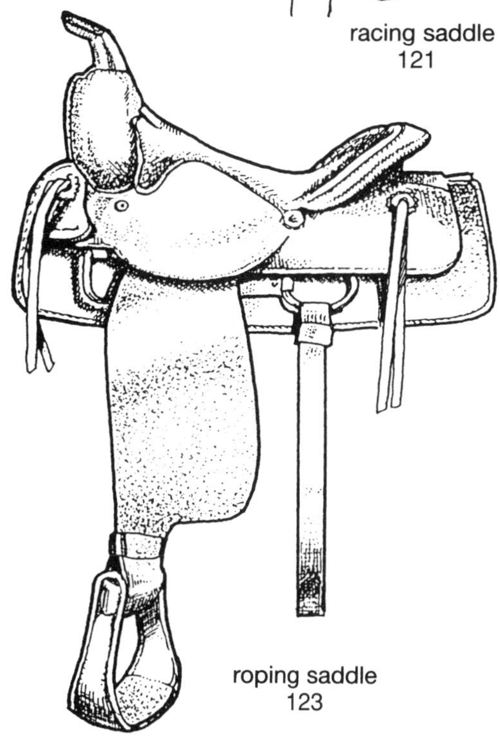

roping saddle
123

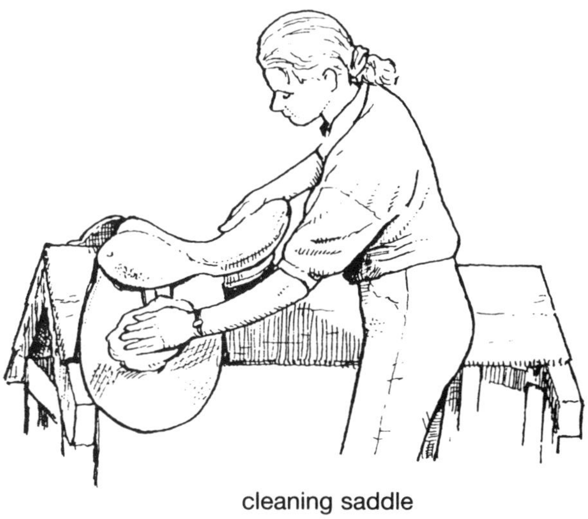

cleaning saddle
122

Stirrups

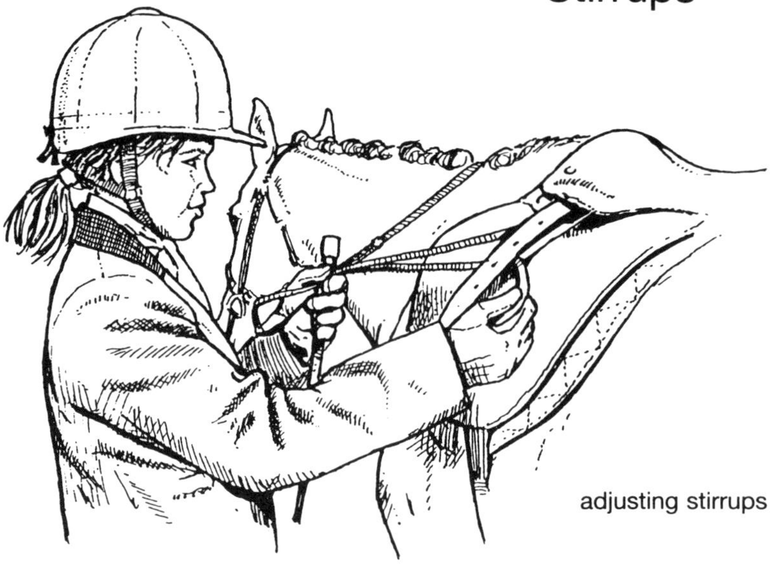

124

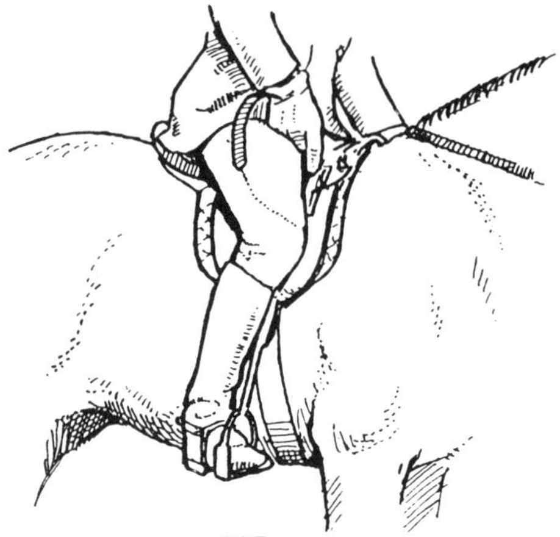

125

adjusting stirrups

Stirrup Irons and Spurs

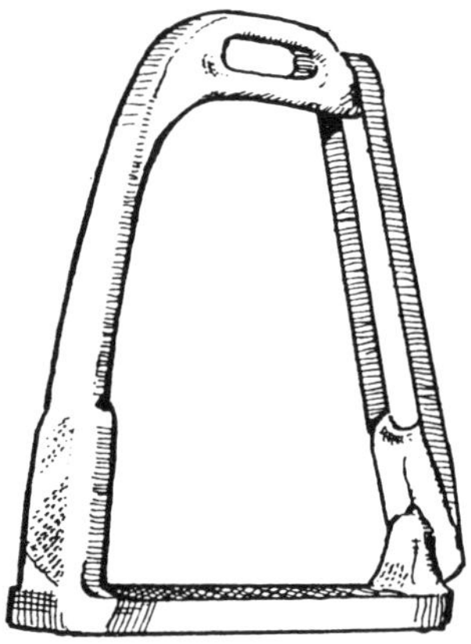

safety iron
126

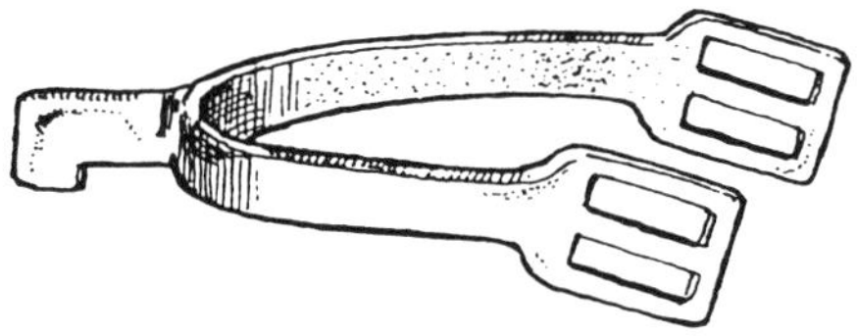

modern spur
127

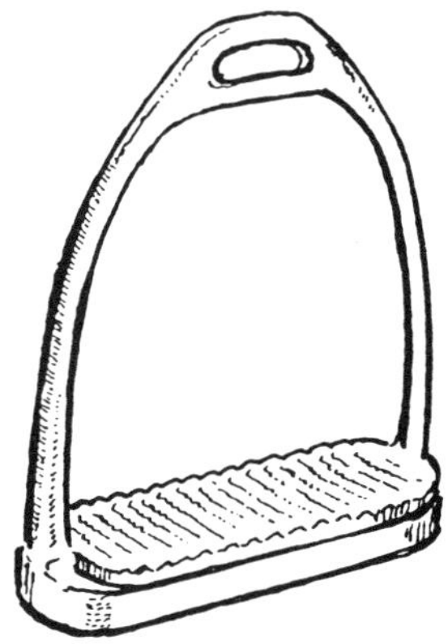

fillis iron with tread
128

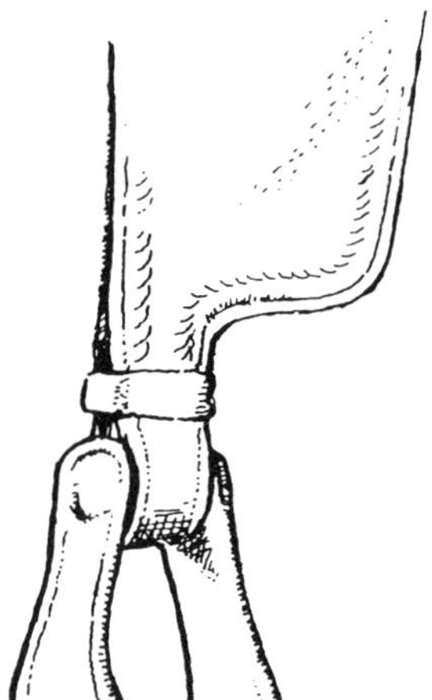

Western stirrup
130

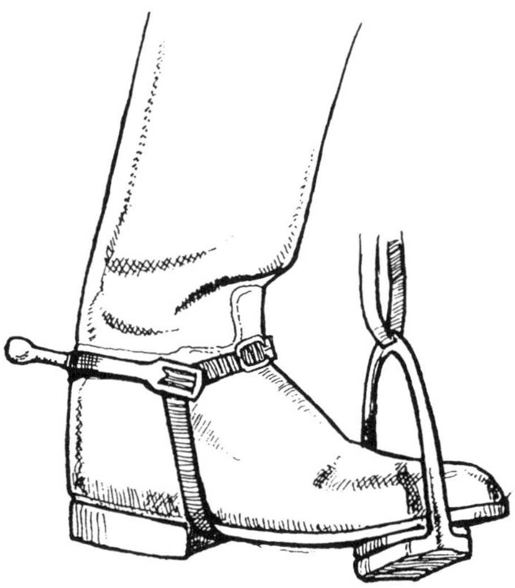

correct position of spur
129

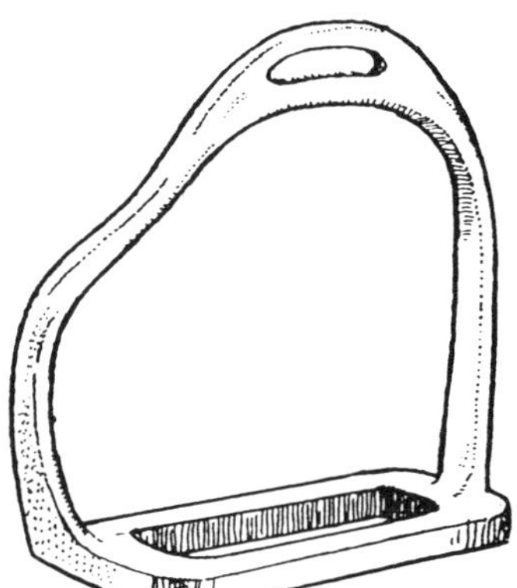

bent leg iron
131

Bits

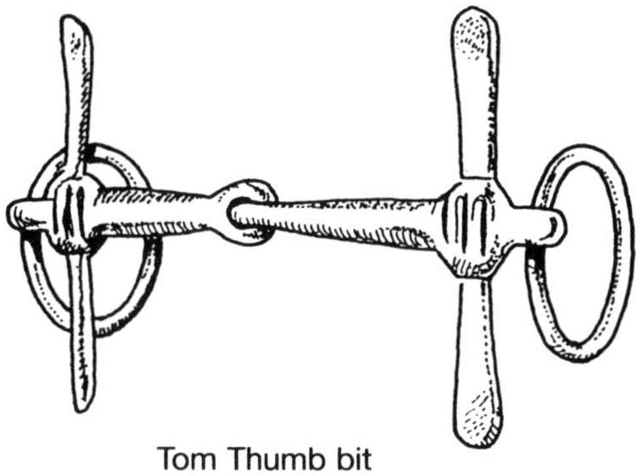

Tom Thumb bit
132

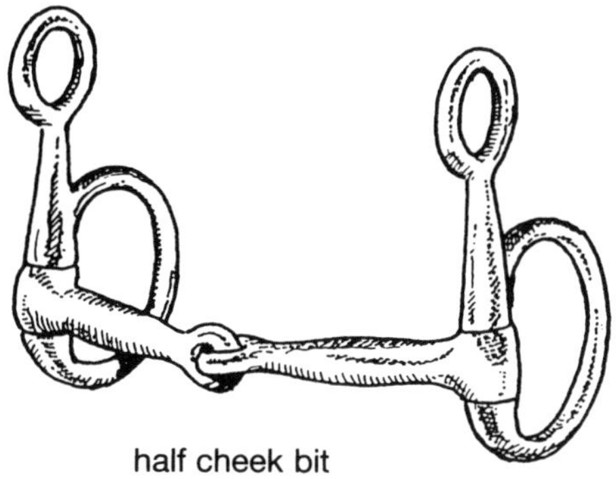

half cheek bit
133

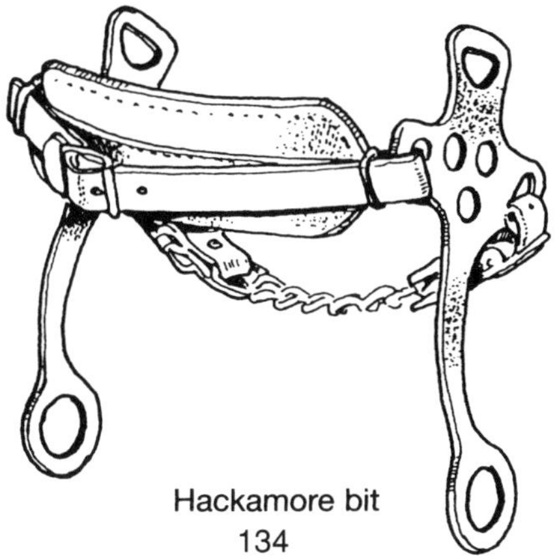

Hackamore bit
134

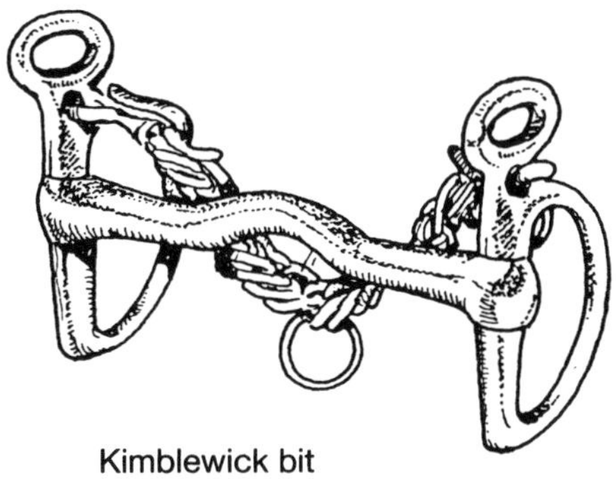

Kimblewick bit
135

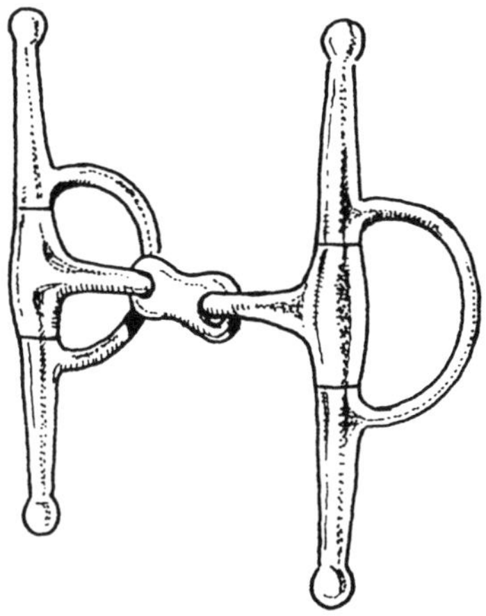

full cheek French link bit
136

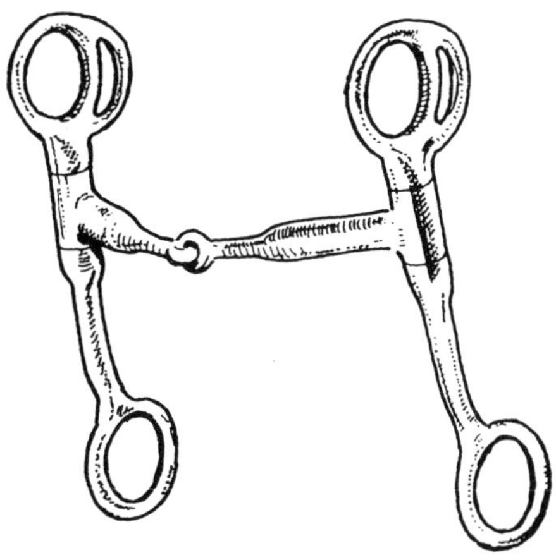

Western Tom Thumb bit (pelham type)
137

The Bridle

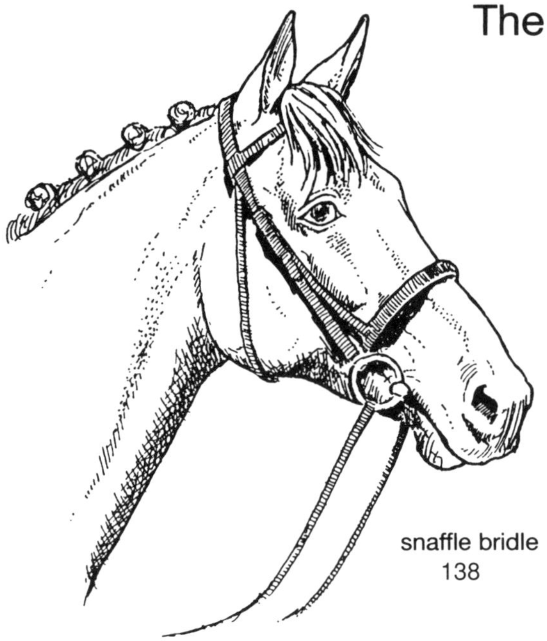

snaffle bridle
138

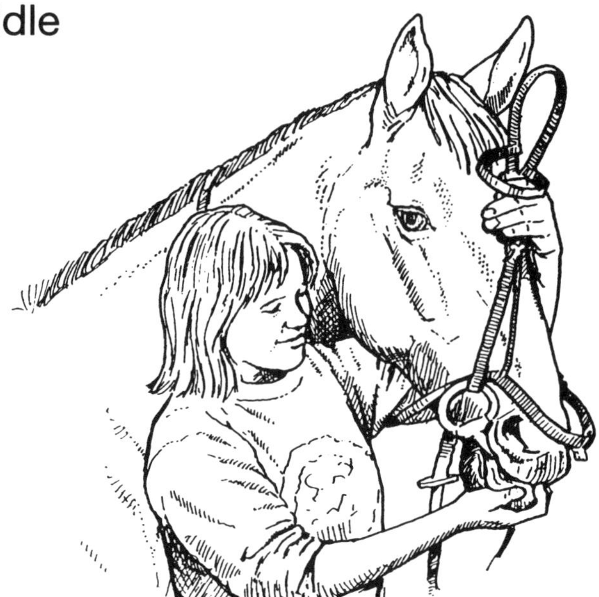

fitting bridle
139

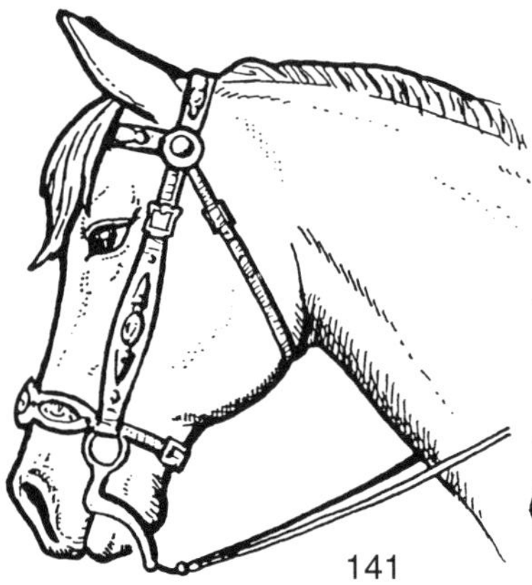

141

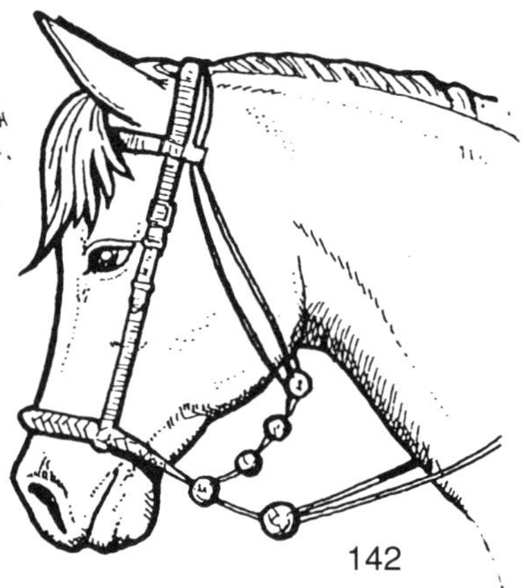

142

Western bridles

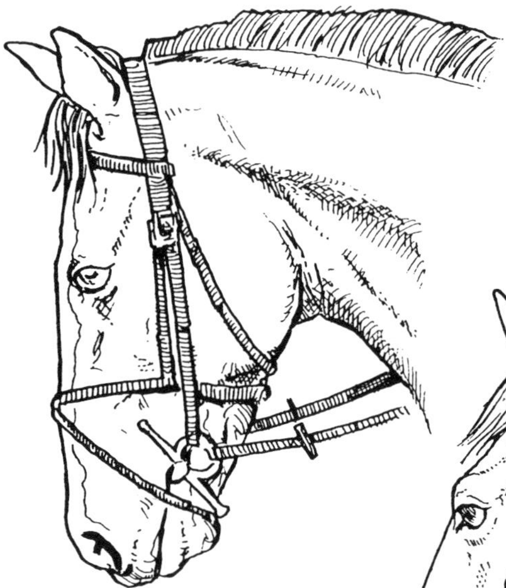

flash bridle
140

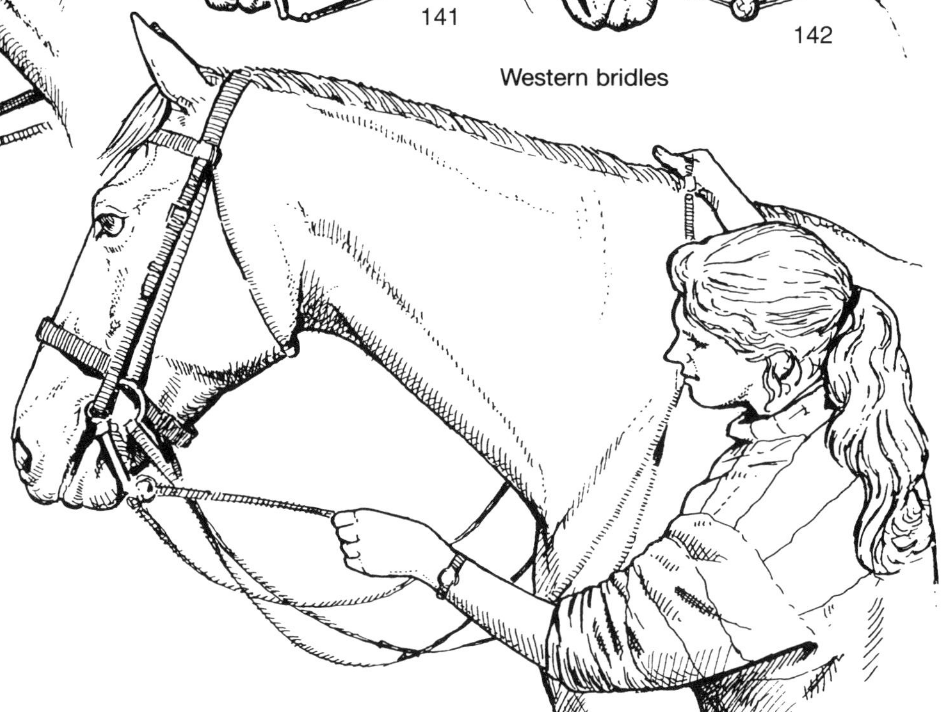

fitting double bridle (weymouth bridle)
143

The Bridle

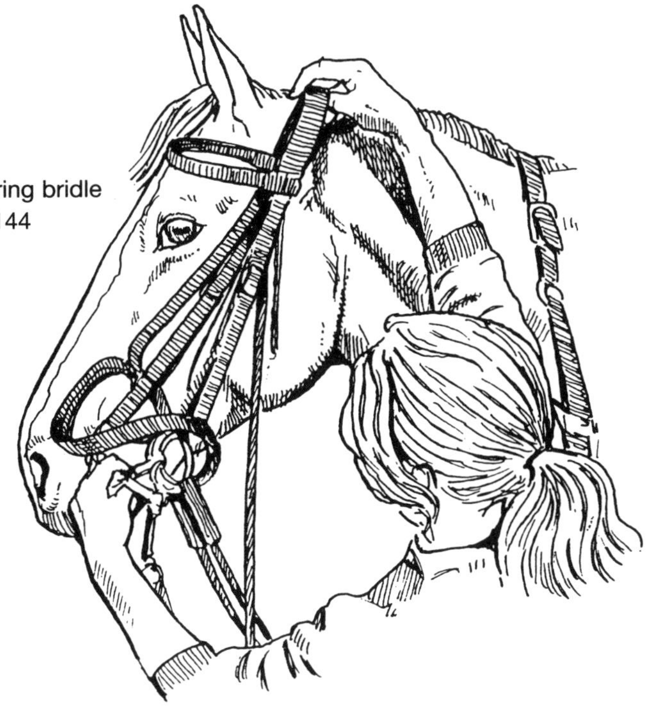

measuring bridle
144

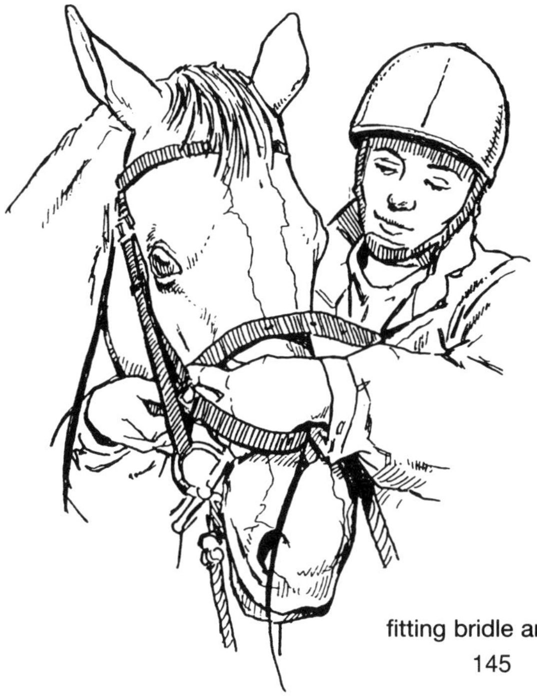

fitting bridle and bit
145

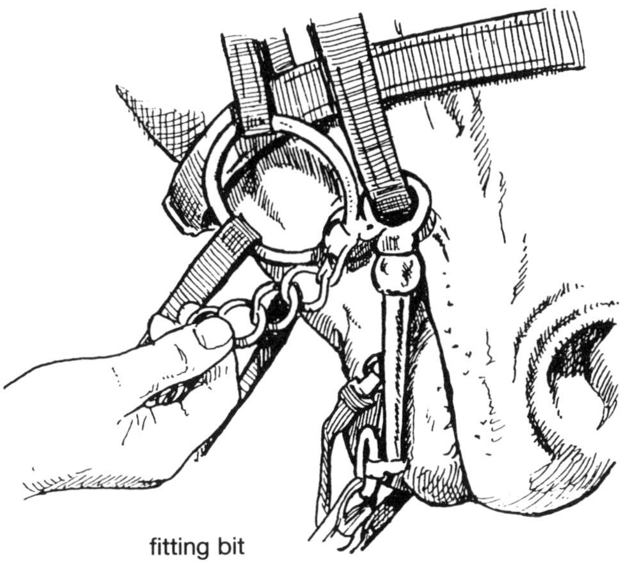

fitting bit
146

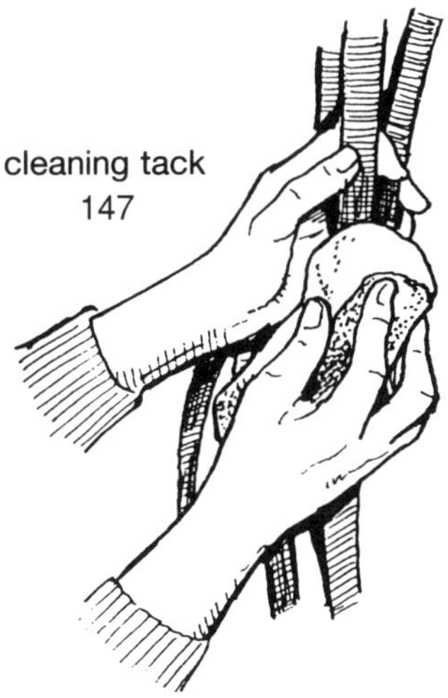

cleaning tack
147

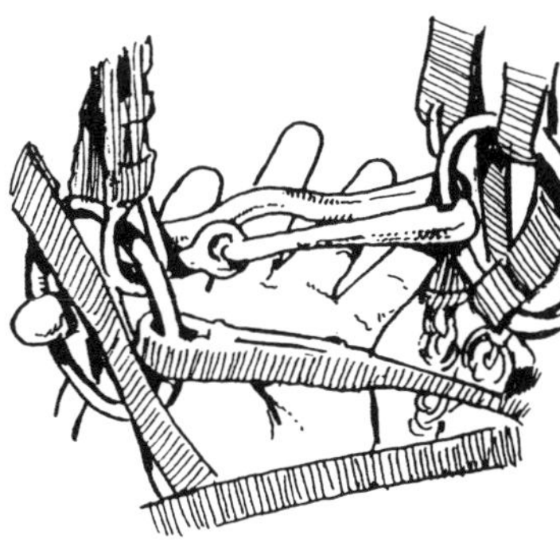

fitting bit
148

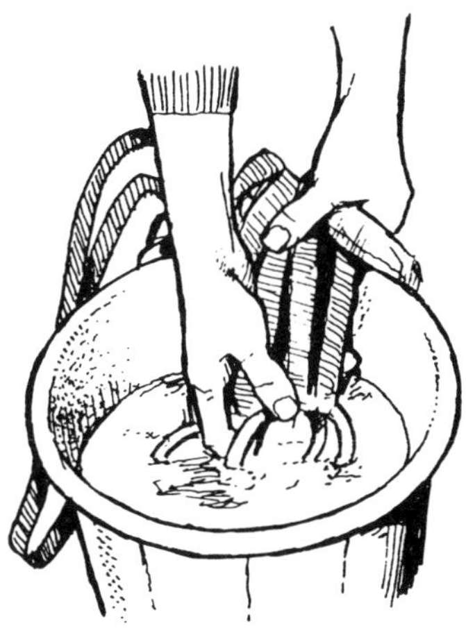

cleaning tack
149

Racing

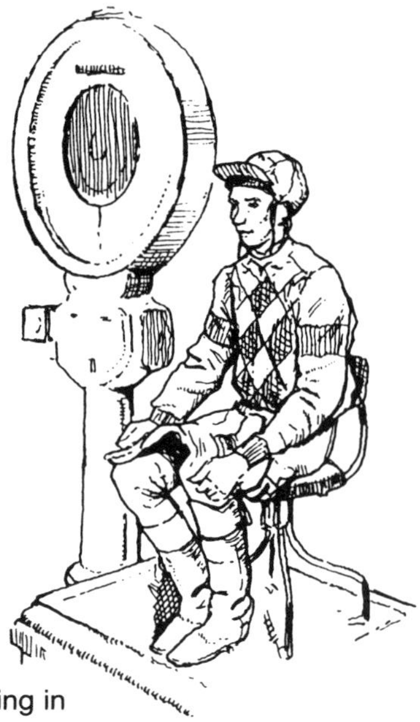

weighing in
150

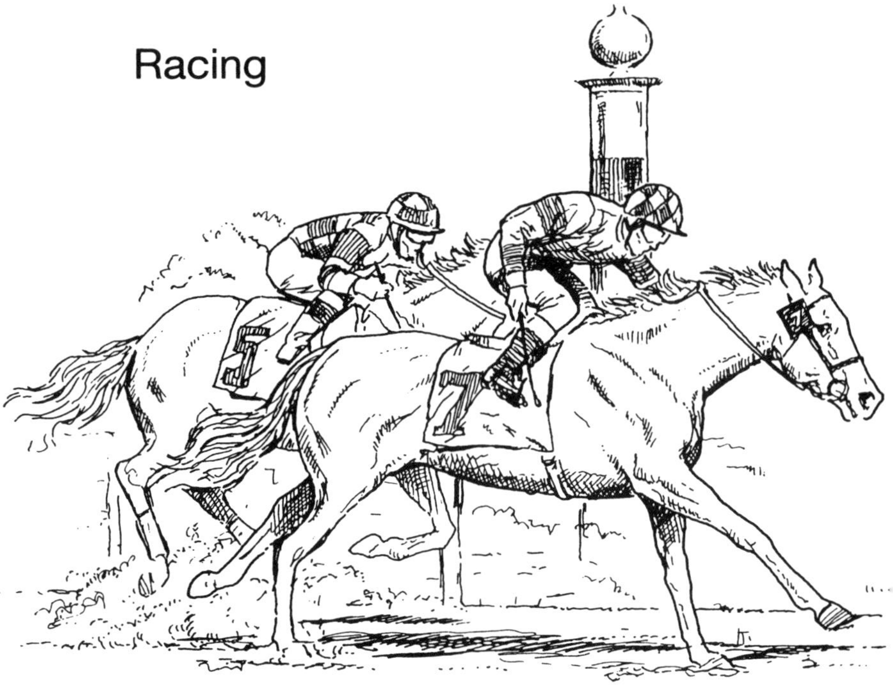

finishing post
151

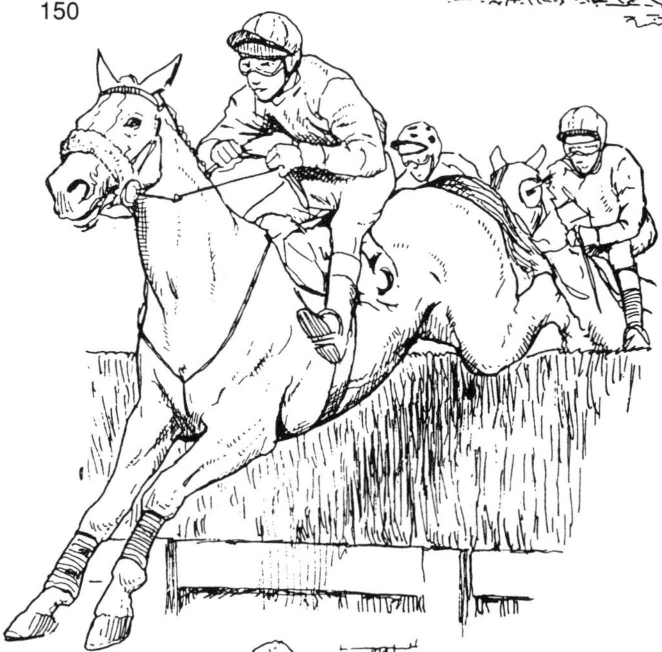

steeplechasing
152

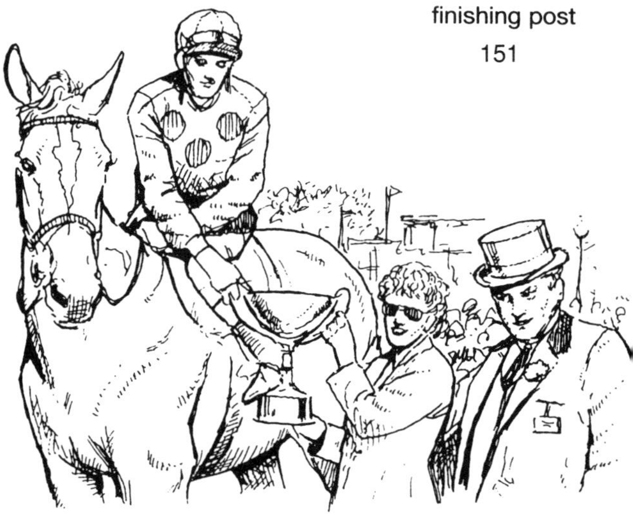

in winner's circle
153

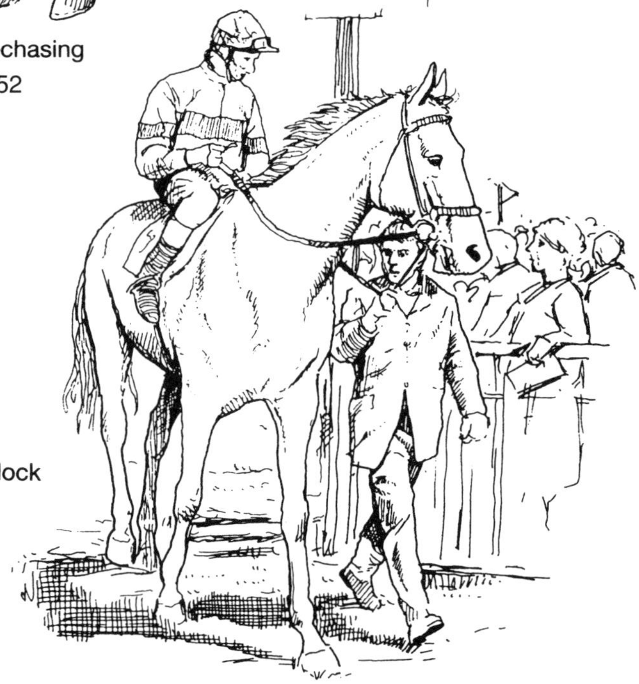

in paddock
154

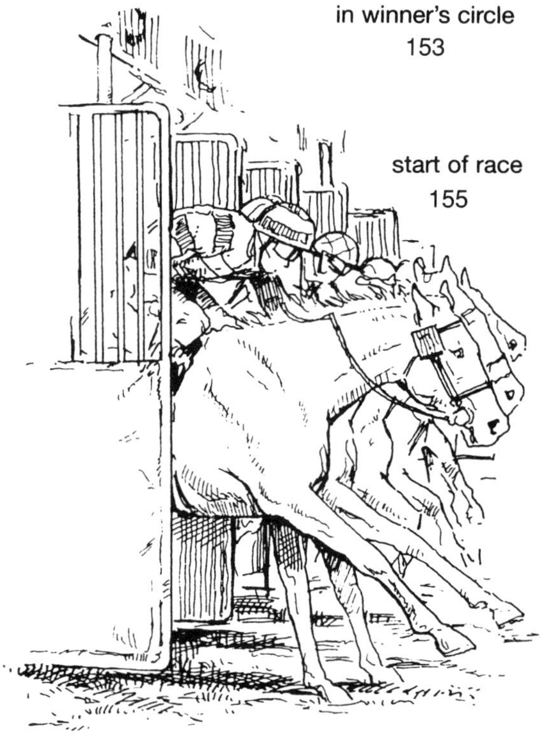

start of race
155

Rodeo

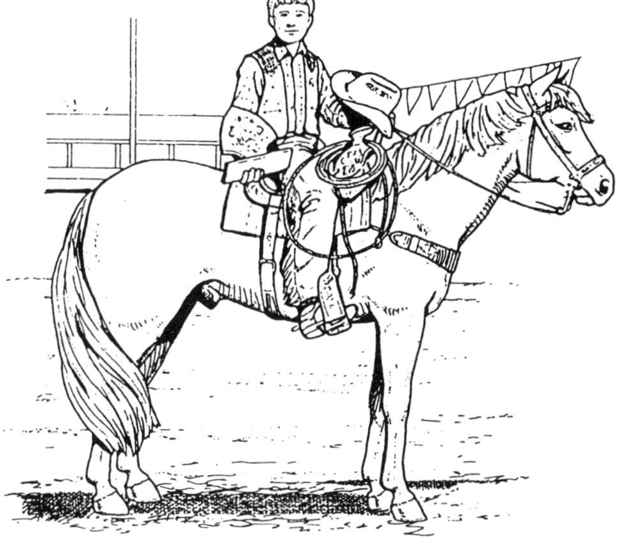

prizewinner
156

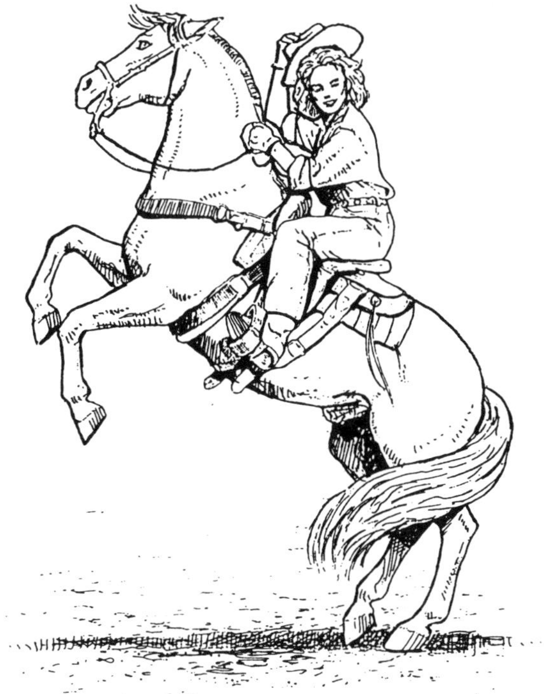

showing
157

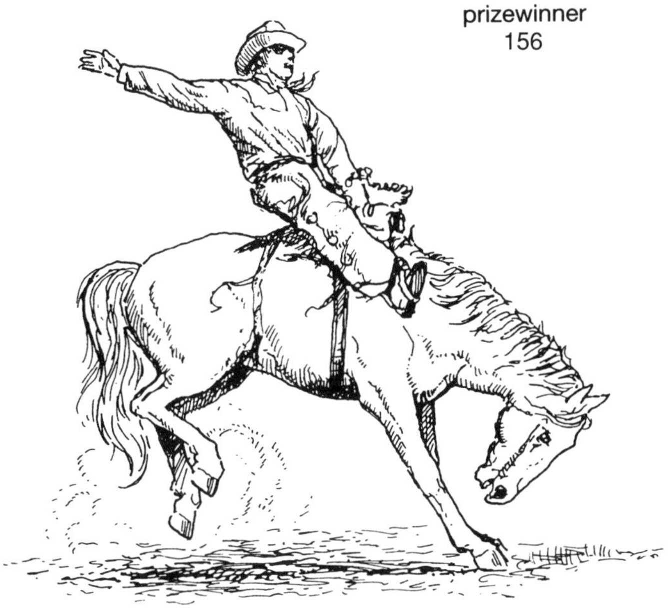

bronco riding
158

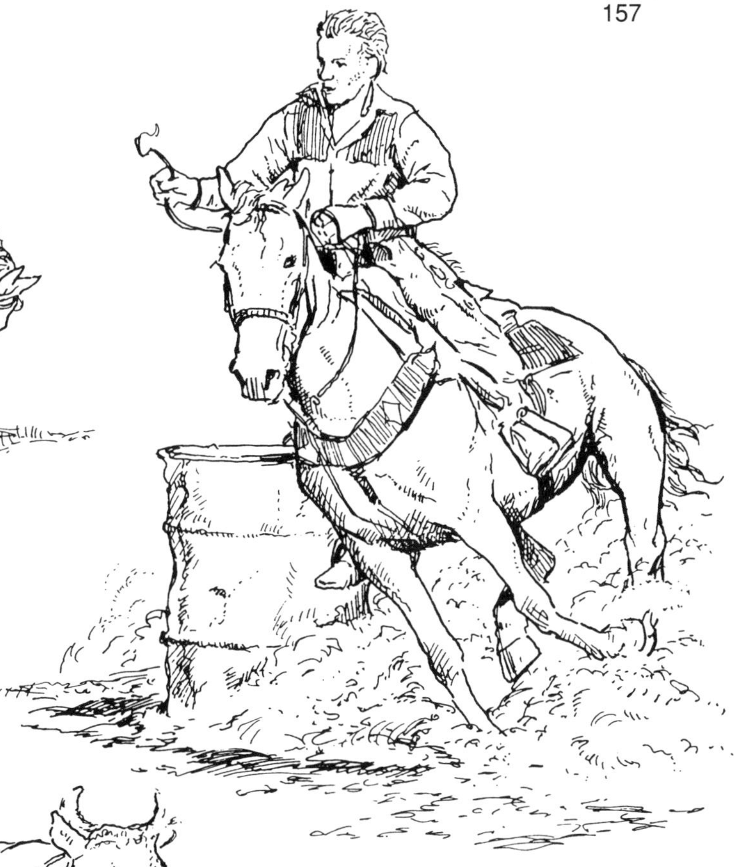

barrel racing
159

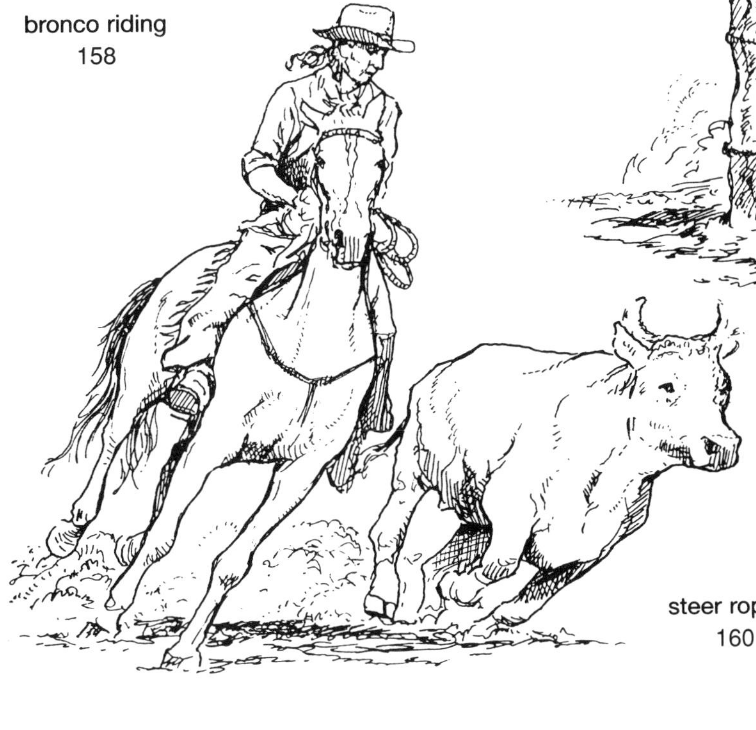

steer roping
160

The Horse in Harness

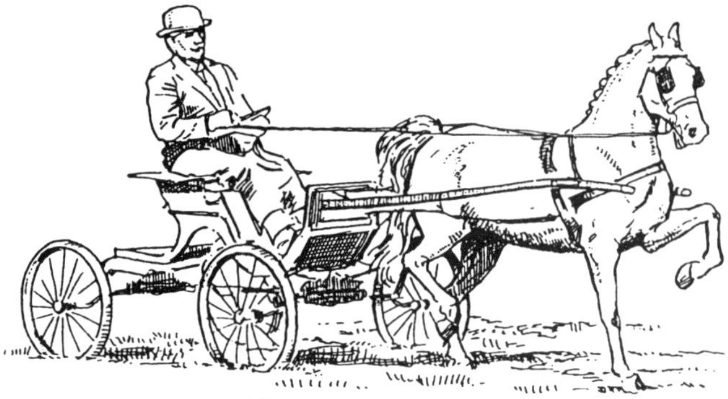

pony and trap
162

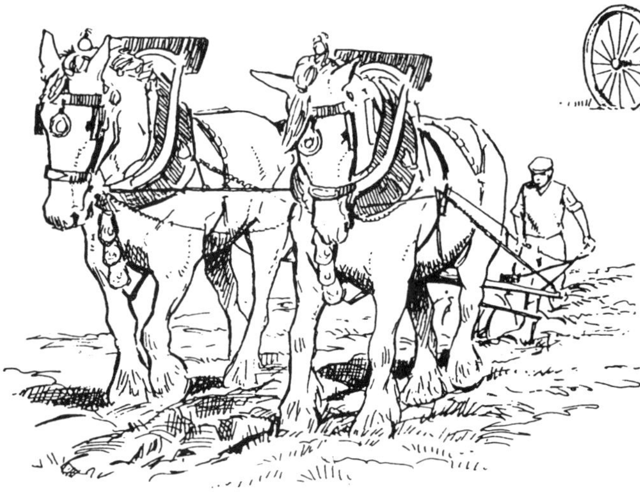

ploughing
161

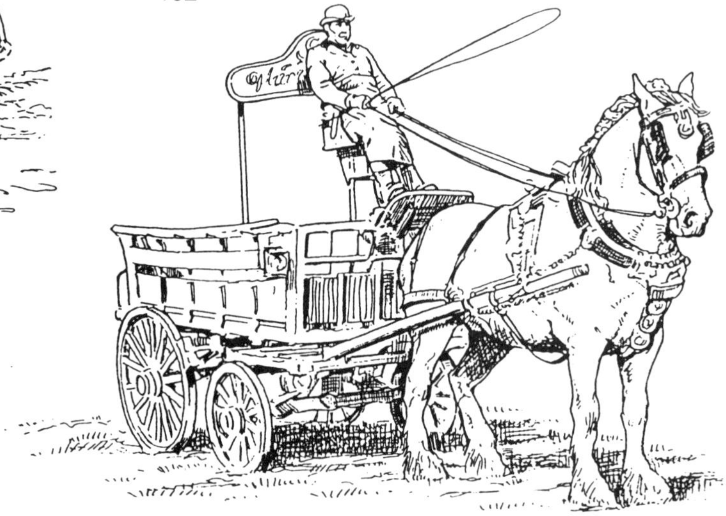

horse and cart
163

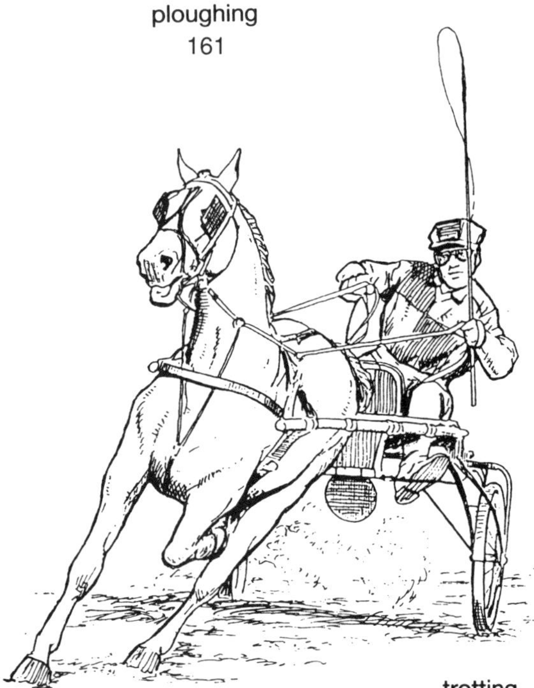

164 trotting

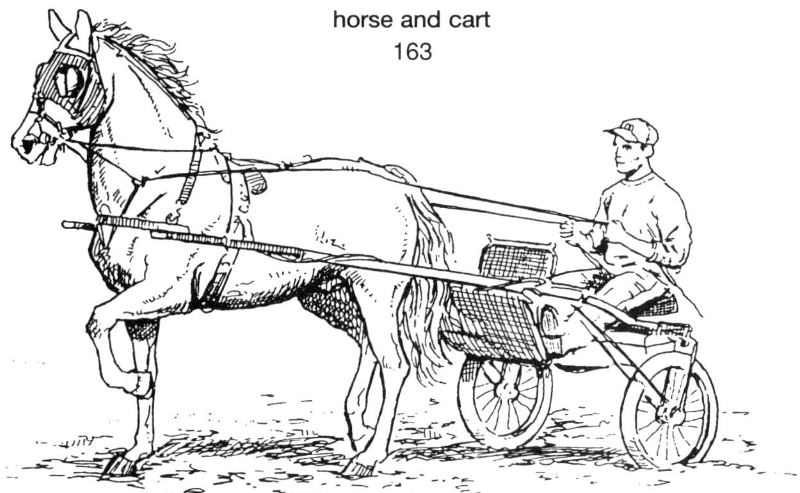

165

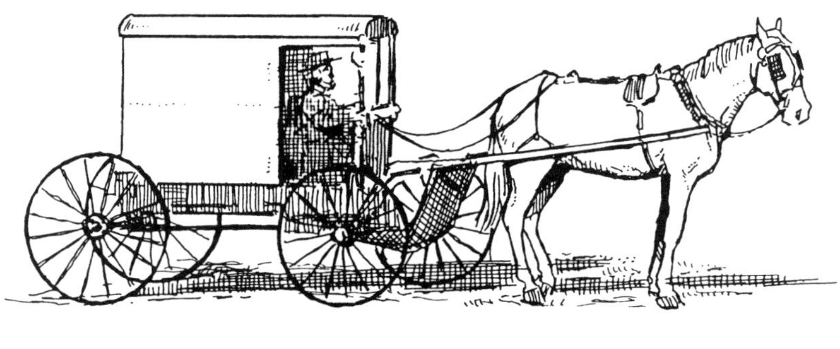

Amish box cart
166

Schooling or Trained Horses

Western schooling pacing
167

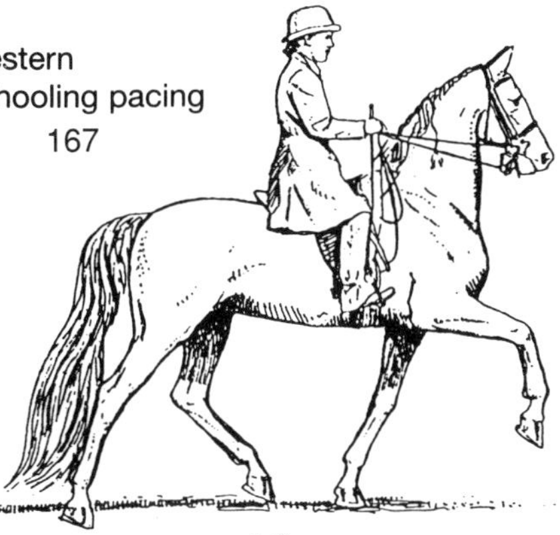

dressage
168

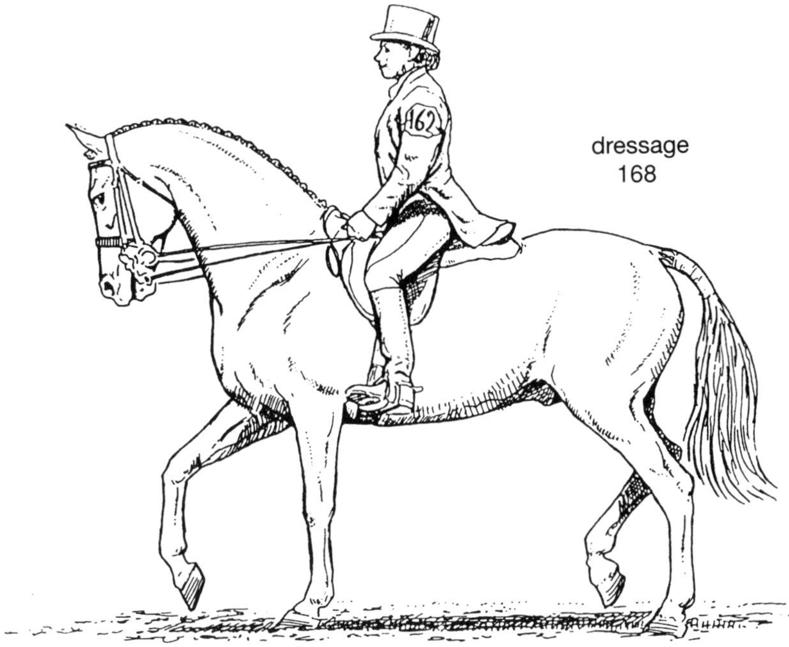

circus horse
169

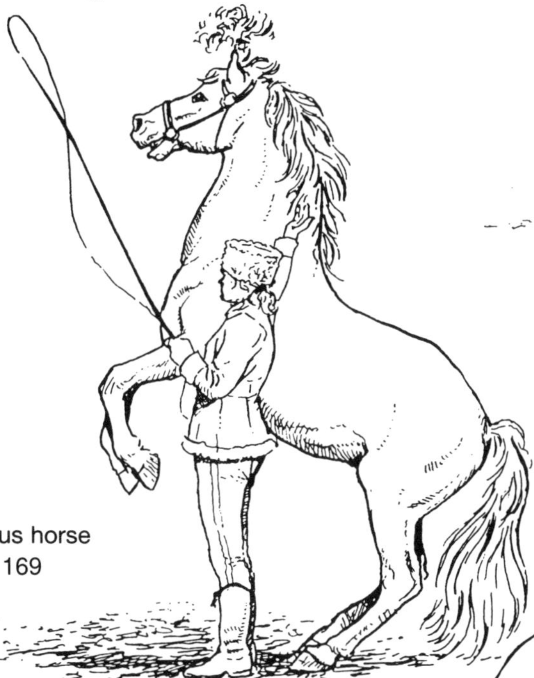

Spanish riding school

170

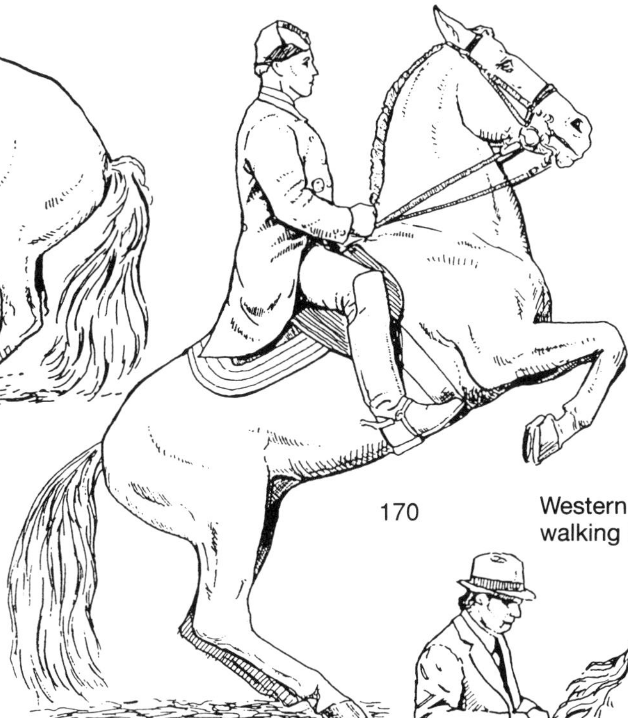

dressage

171

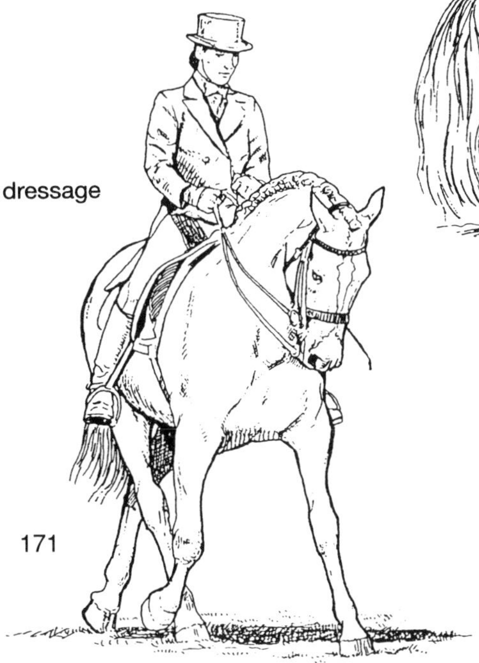

Western schooling, Tennessee walking horse

172

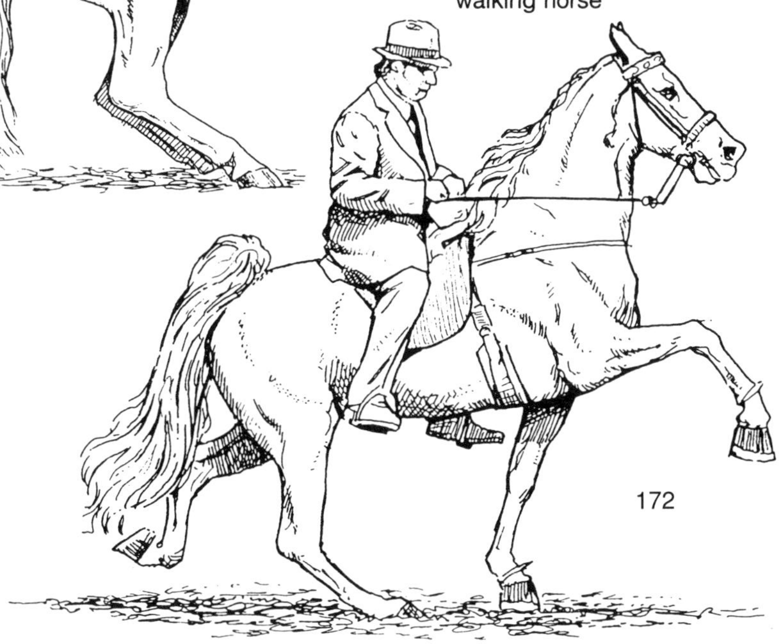

Show Jumping and Showing

wall jump
173

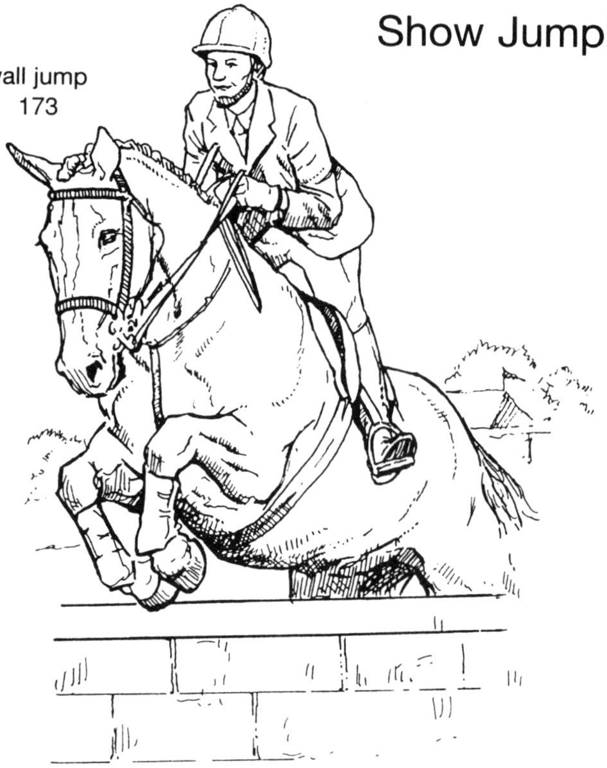

triple bar jump—upright
174

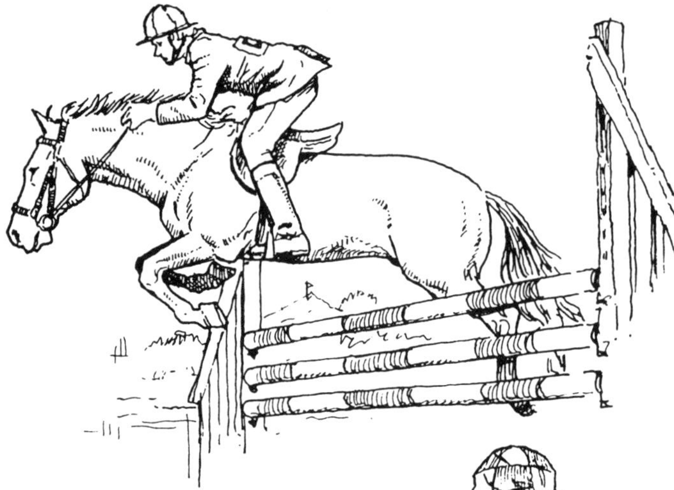

cross bar jump
176

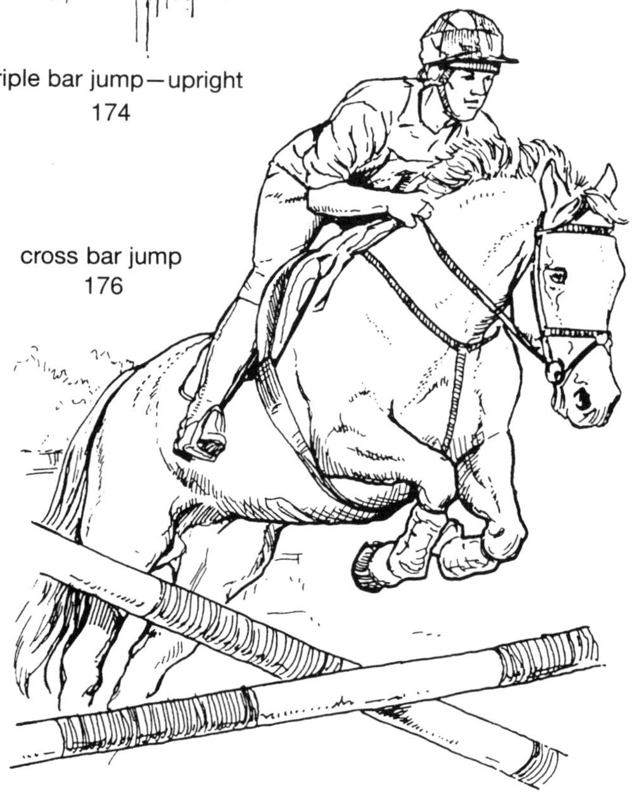

prizewinner
175

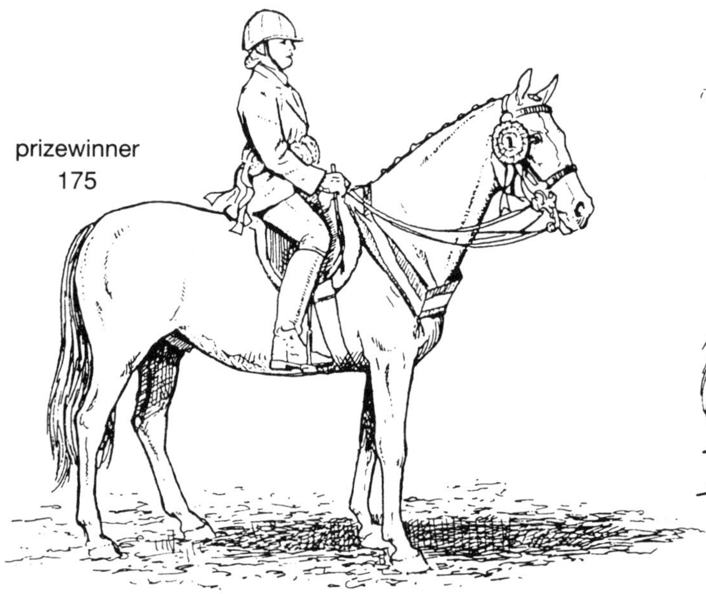

double bar
jump spread
177

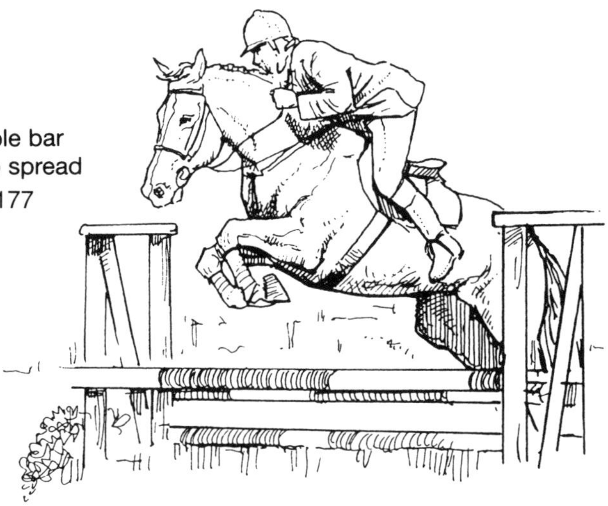

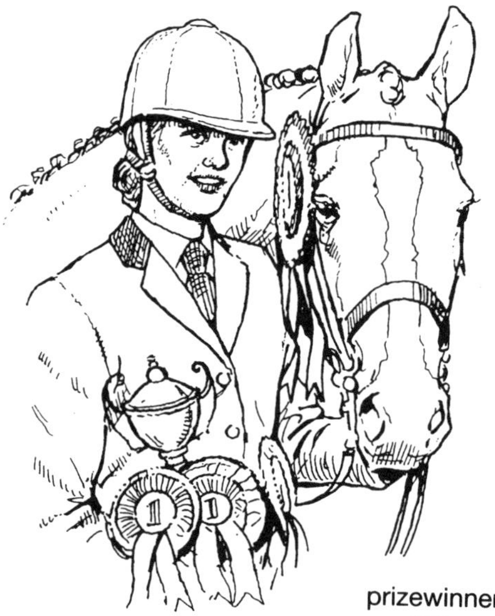

prizewinner
178

Cross-Country Jumping

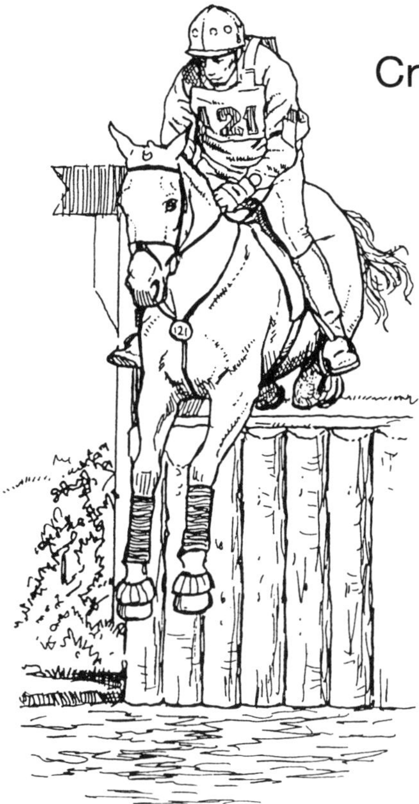

water jump
179

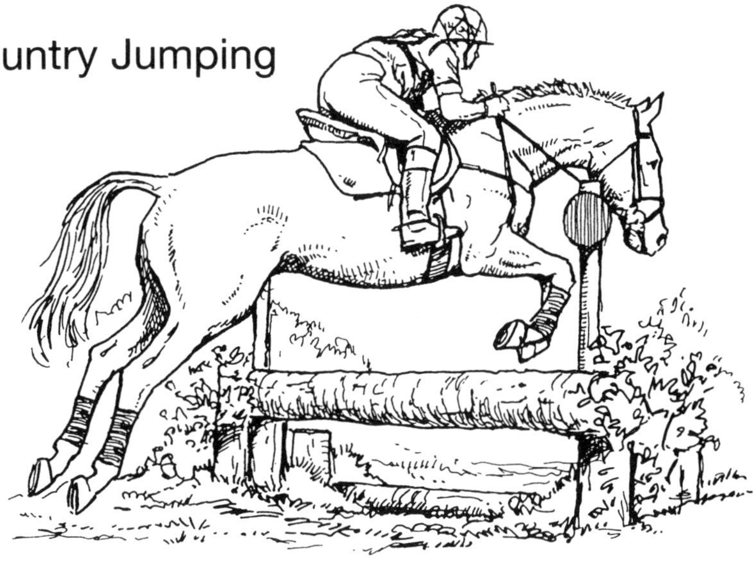

jumping over tree trunk
180

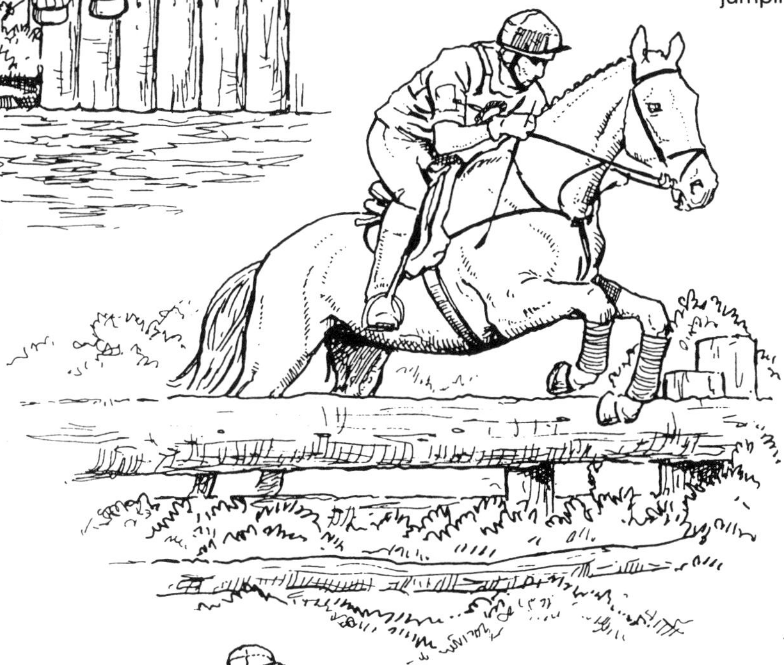

jumping over tree trunk
181

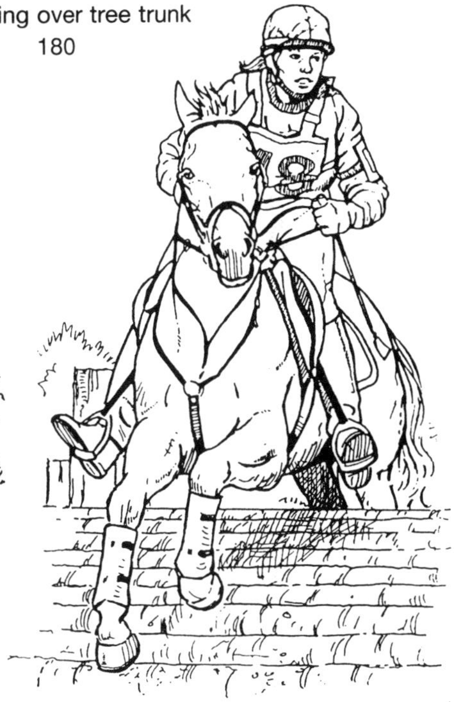

bank jump
182

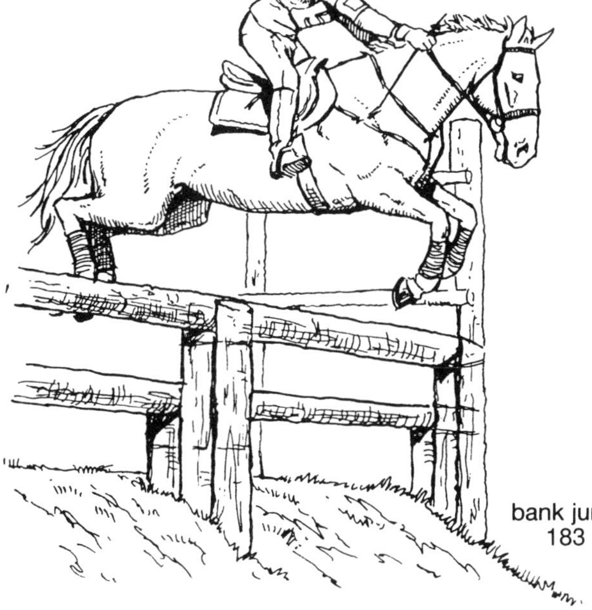

bank jump
183

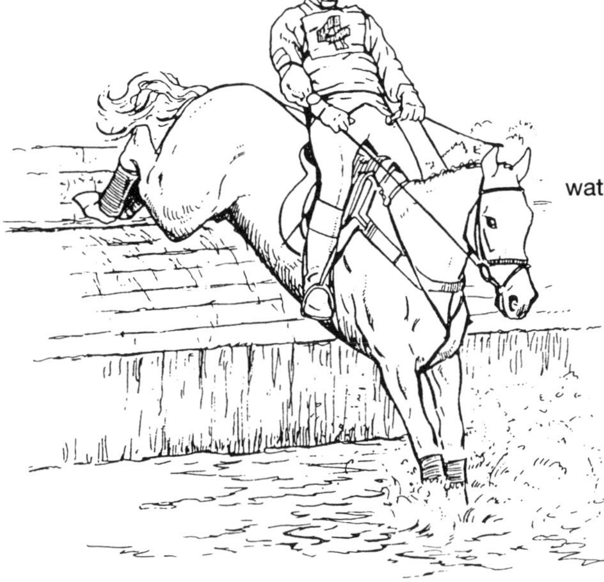

water jump
184

Polo and Hunting

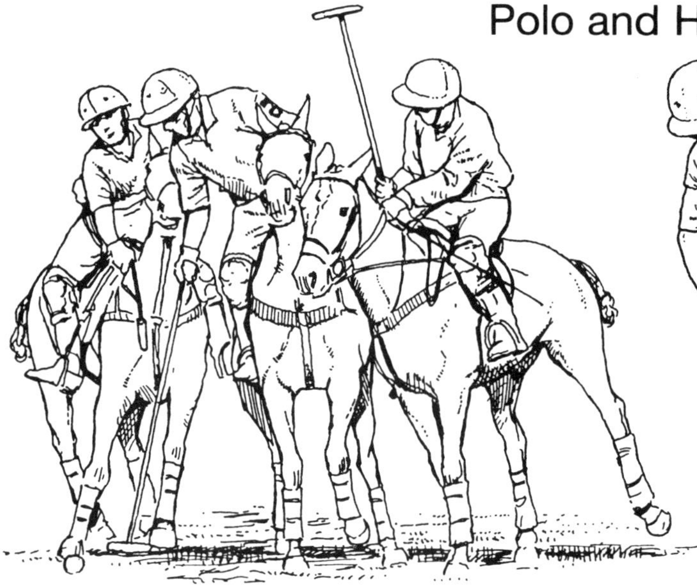

185

polo

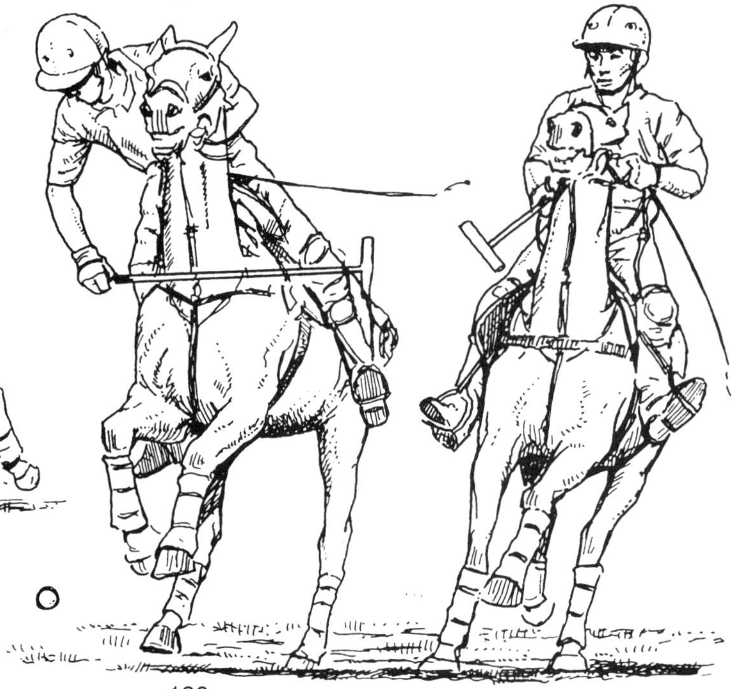

186

polo player

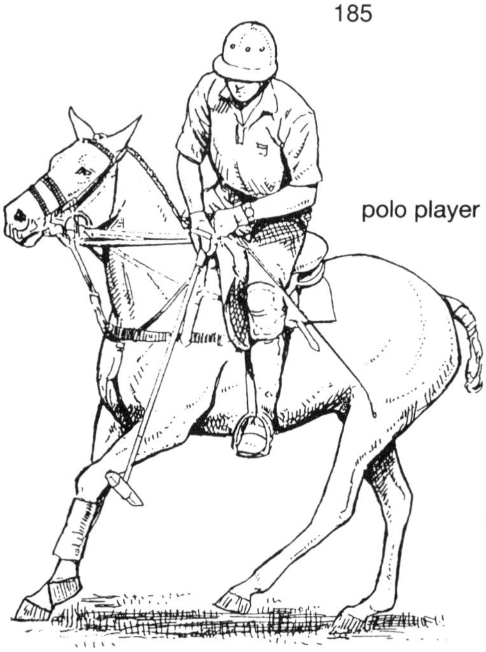

187

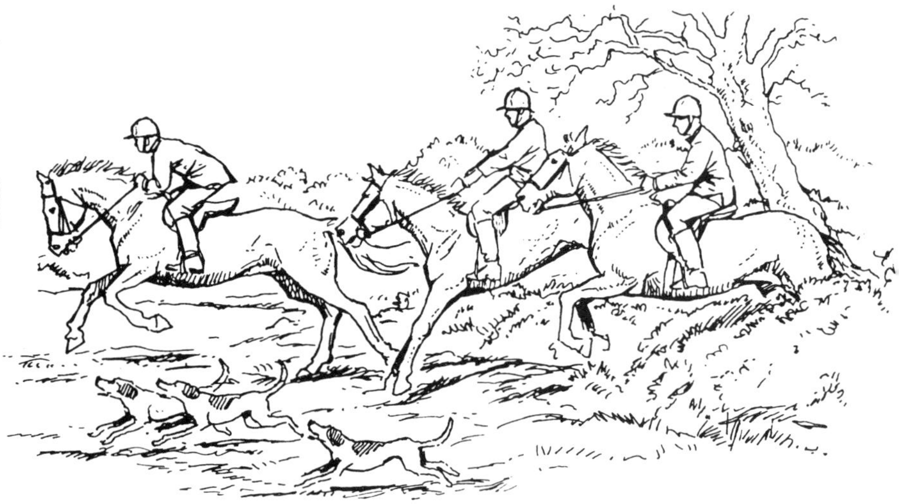

188

foxhunting scenes

189

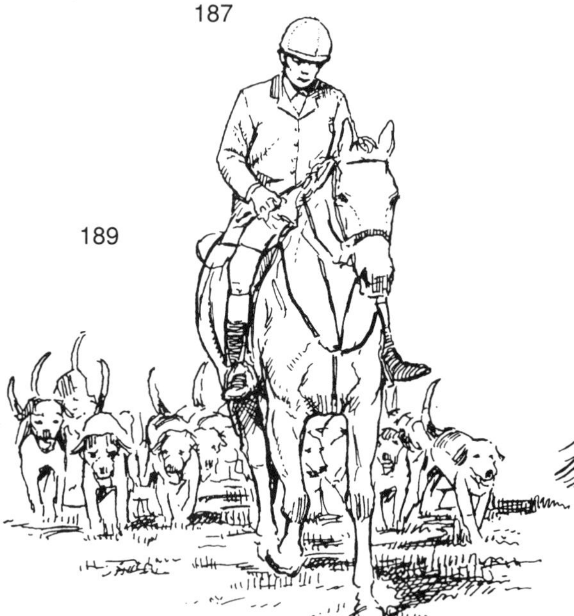

190

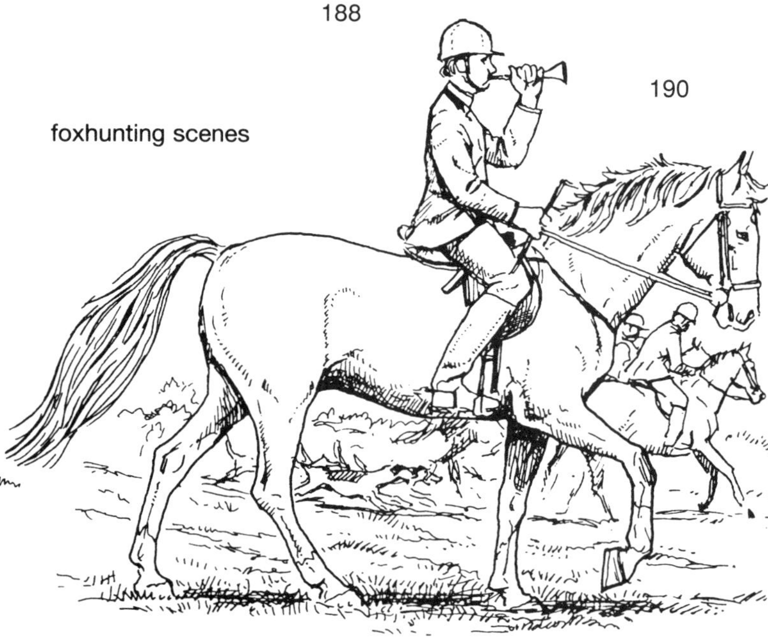

Sport Horses

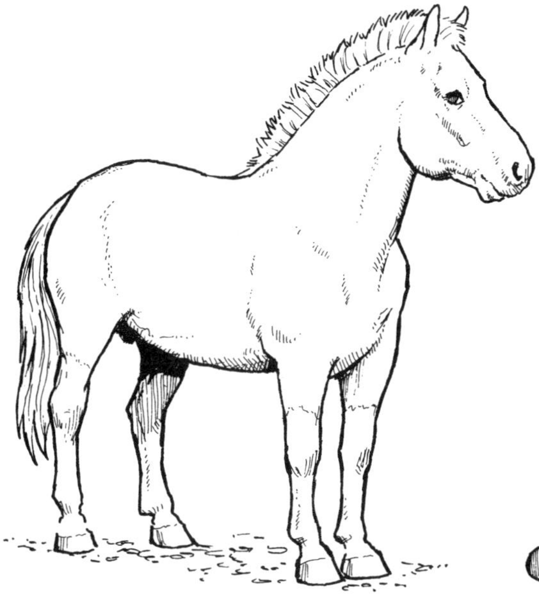

Przewalski's Horse
(wild horse)
191

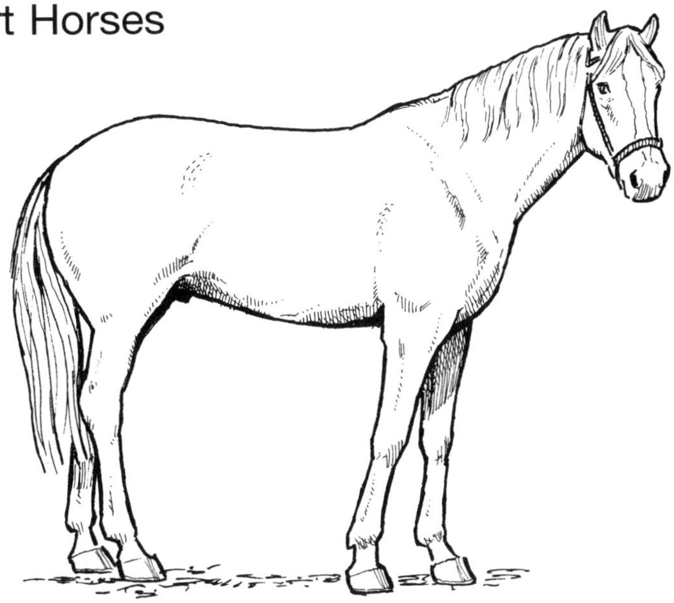

Budyonny
192

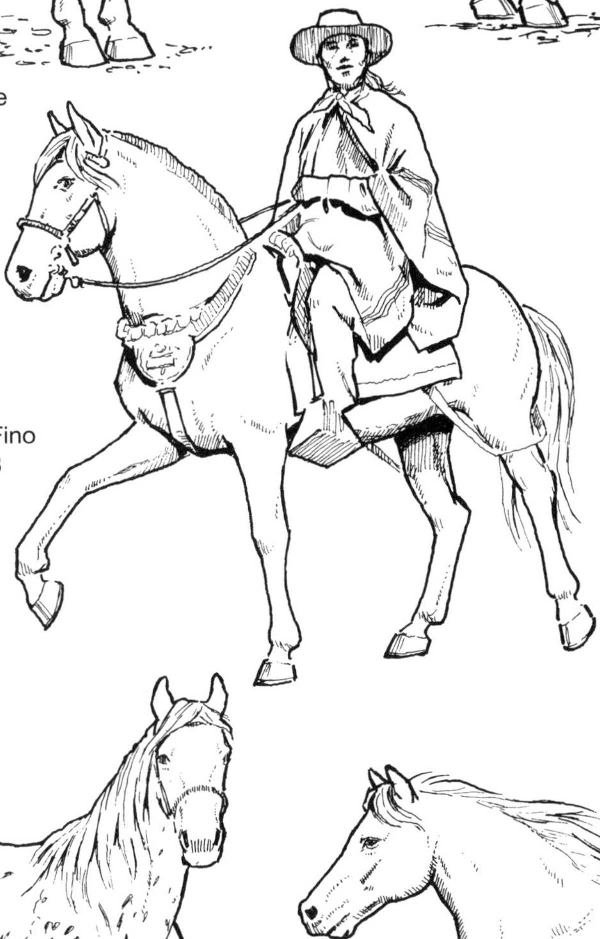

Paso Fino
193

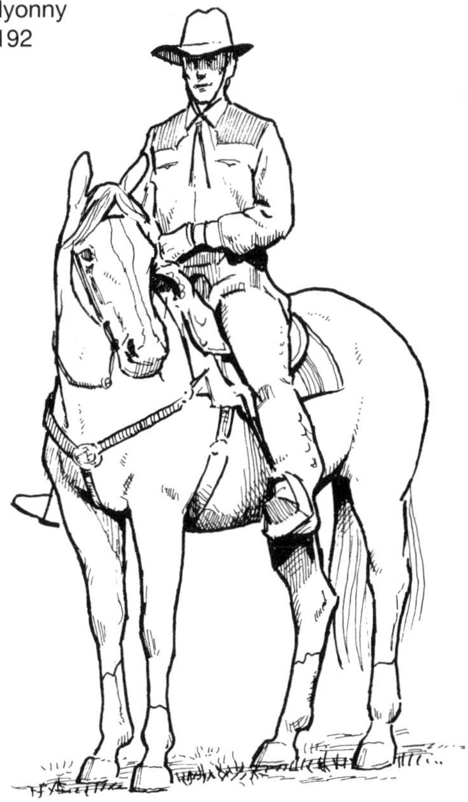

Quarter Horse
194

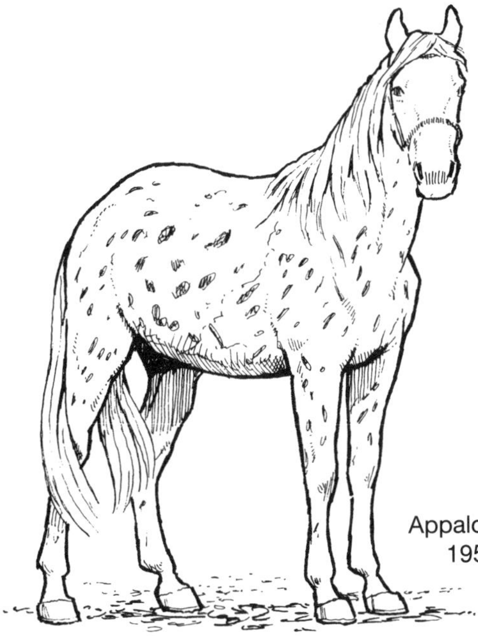

Appaloosa
195

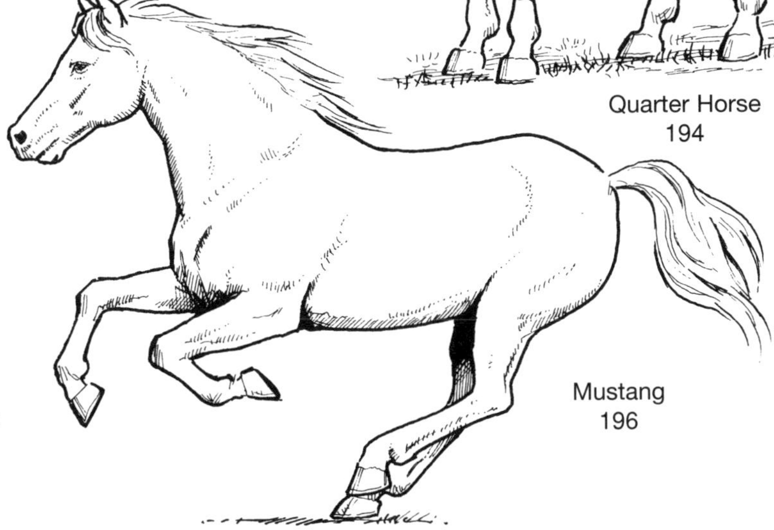

Mustang
196

Sport Horses

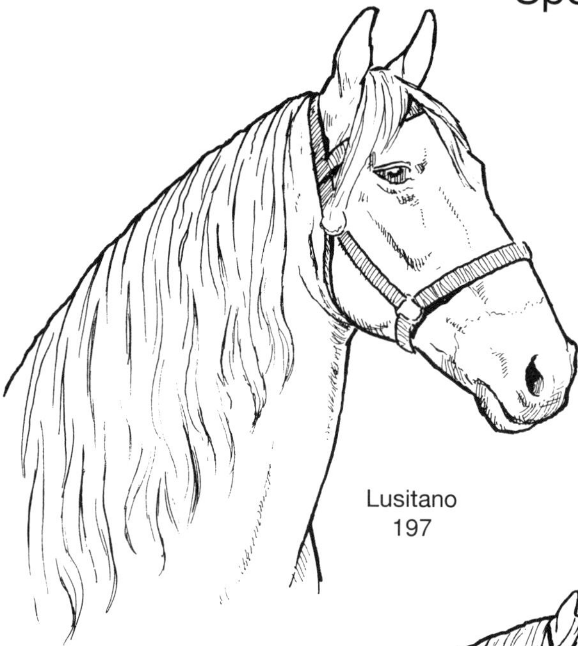

Lusitano
197

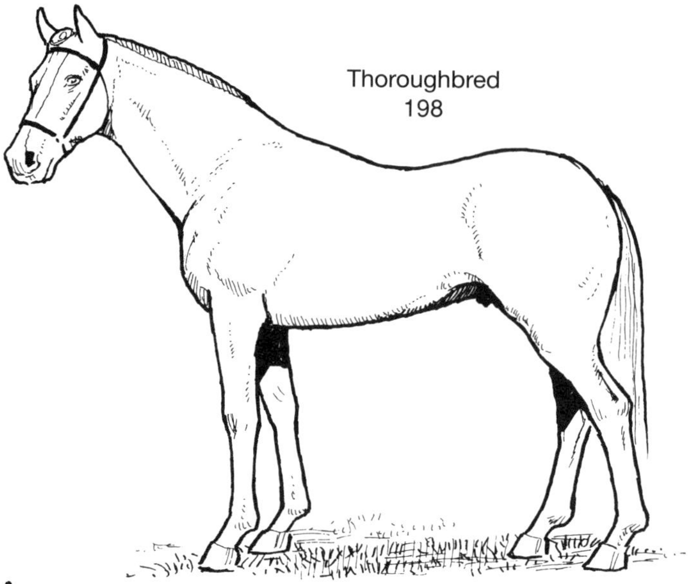

Thoroughbred
198

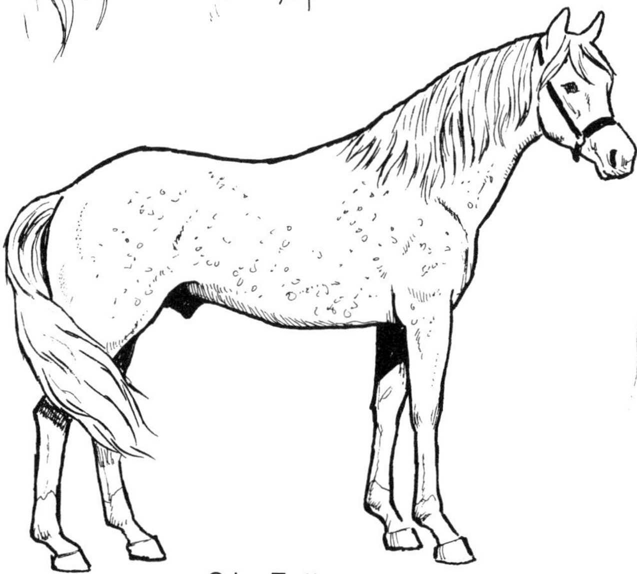

Orlov Trotter
199

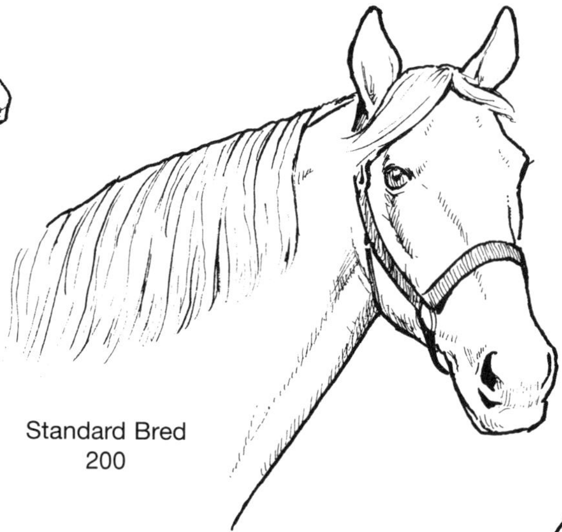

Standard Bred
200

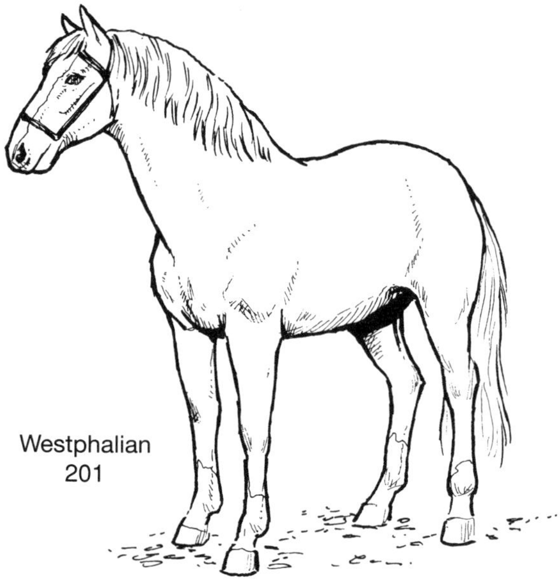

Westphalian
201

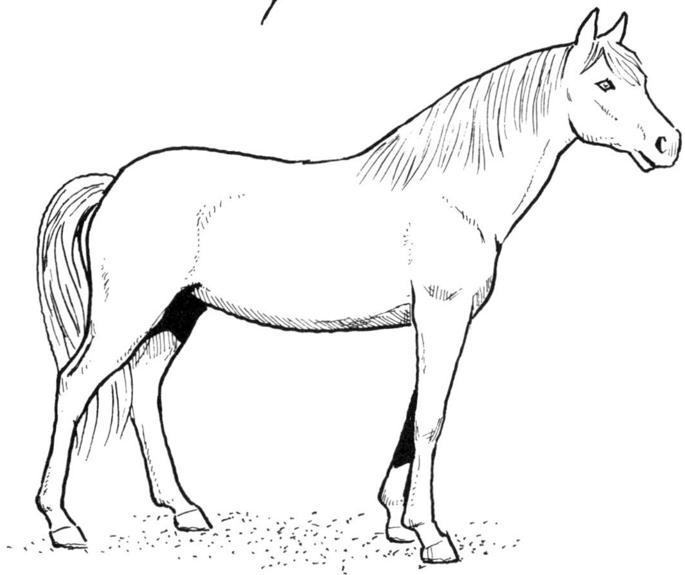

Furioso
202

Sport Horses

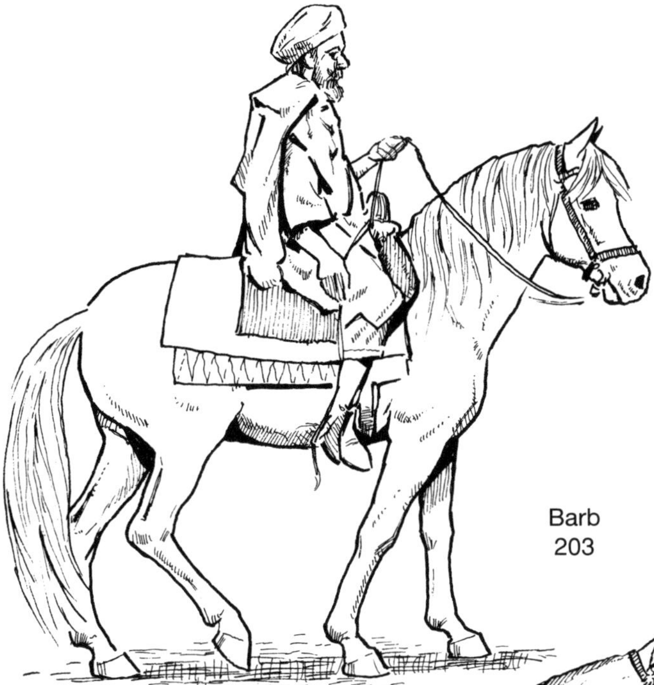

Barb
203

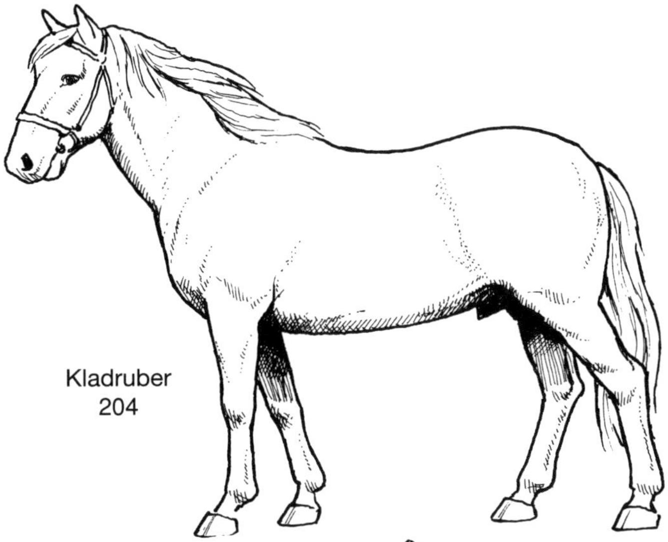

Kladruber
204

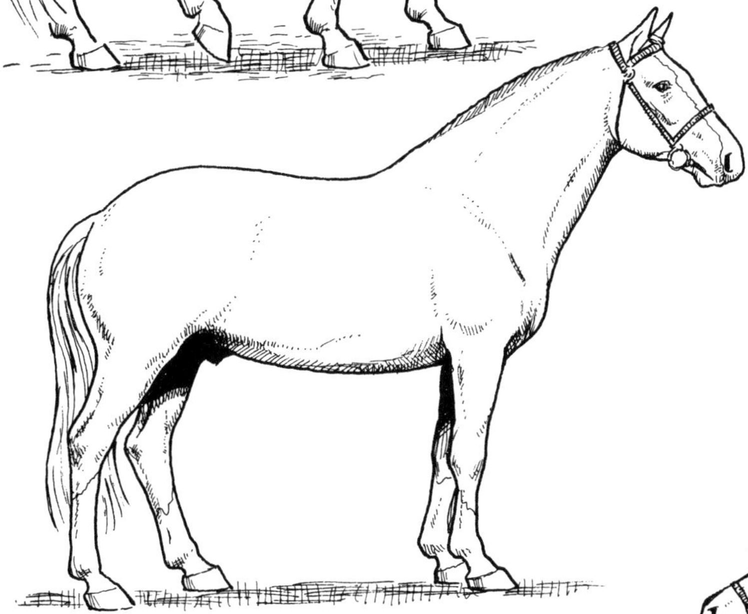

Cob
205

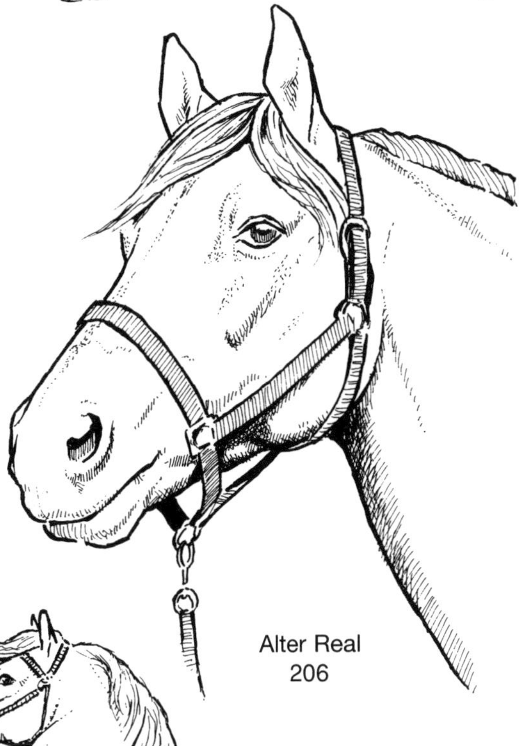

Alter Real
206

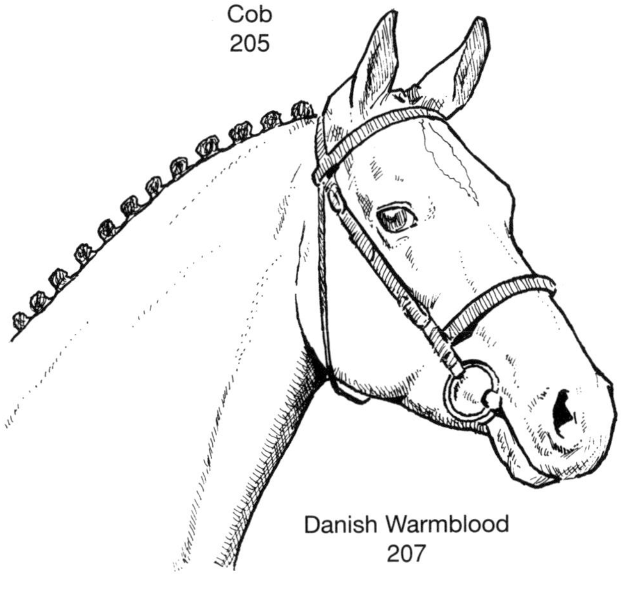

Danish Warmblood
207

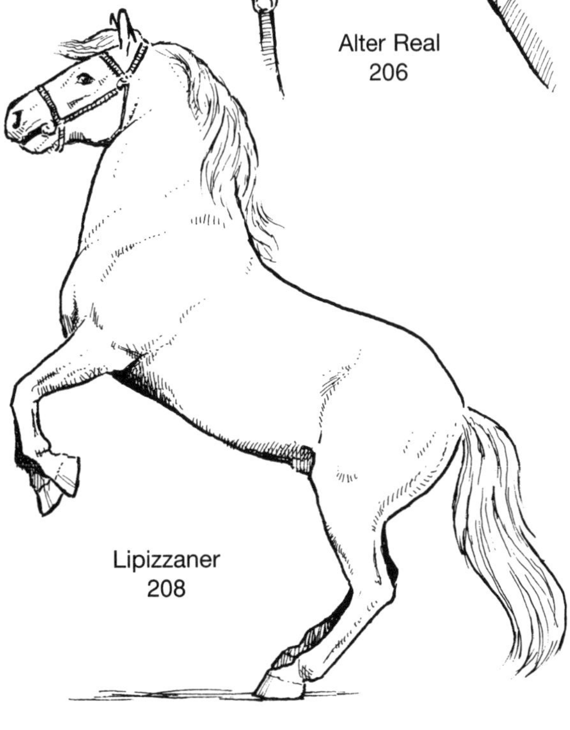

Lipizzaner
208

Sport Horses

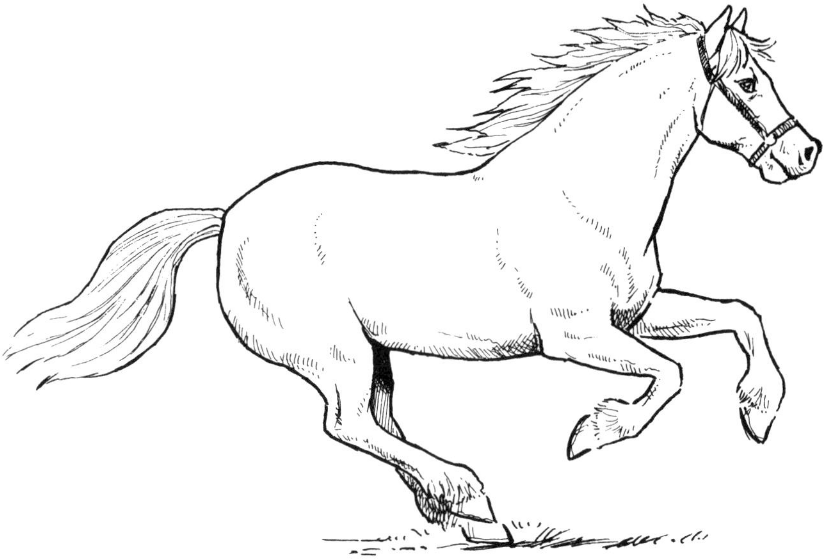

Fresian
209

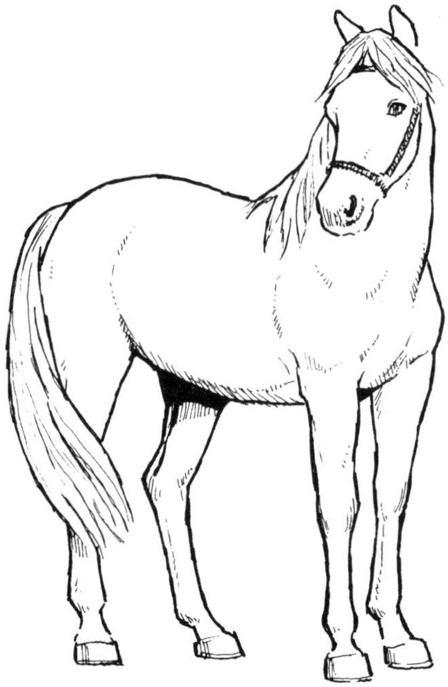

Morgan
210

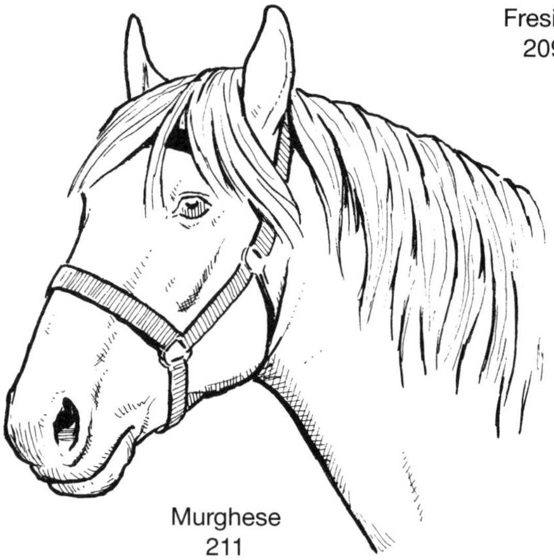

Murghese
211

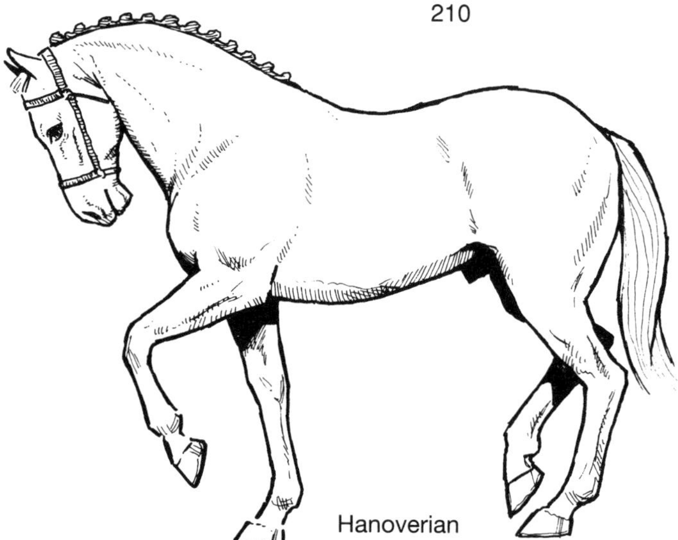

Hanoverian
212

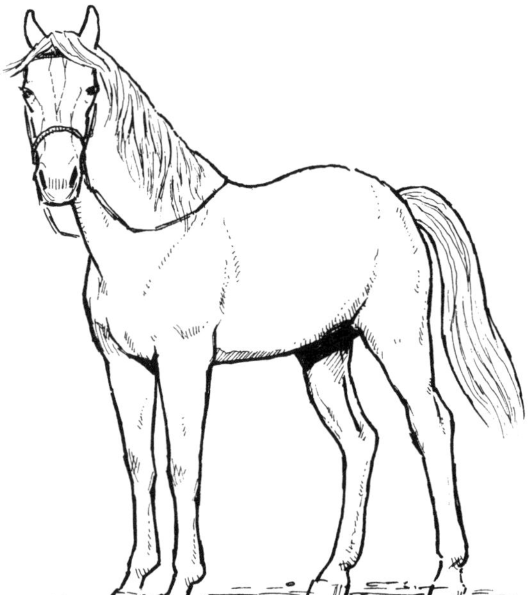

Rocky Mountain Pony
213

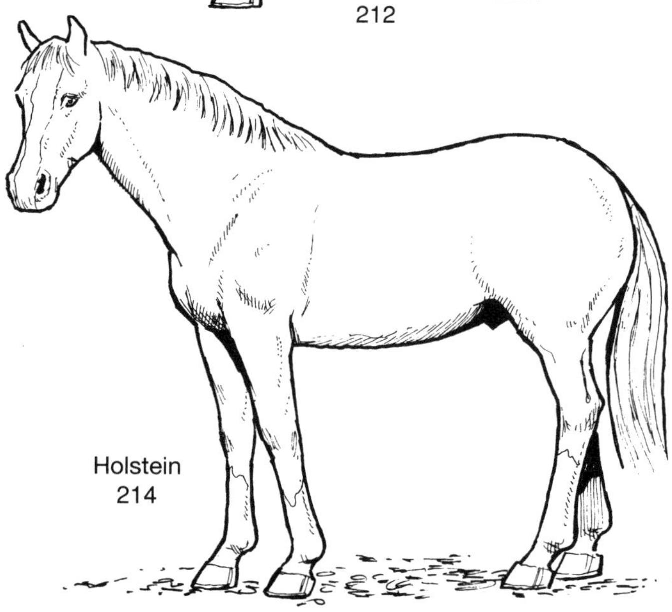

Holstein
214

Sport Horses

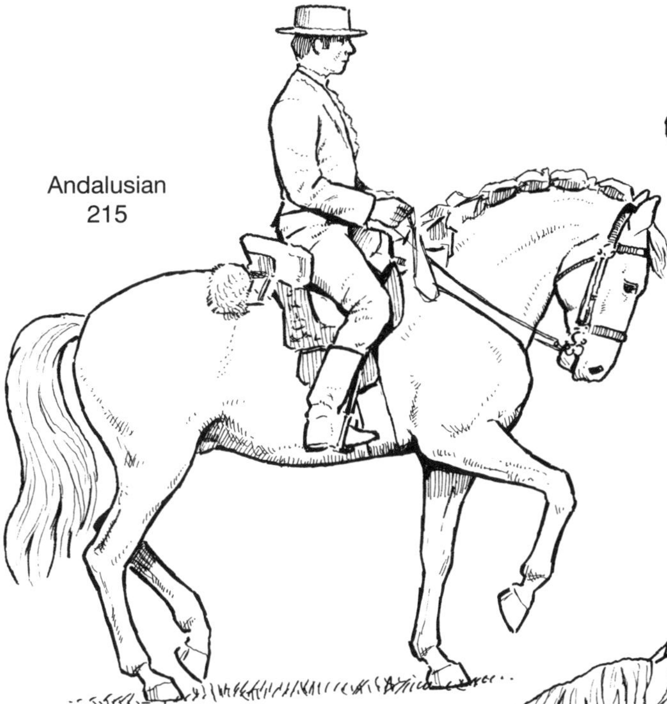

Andalusian
215

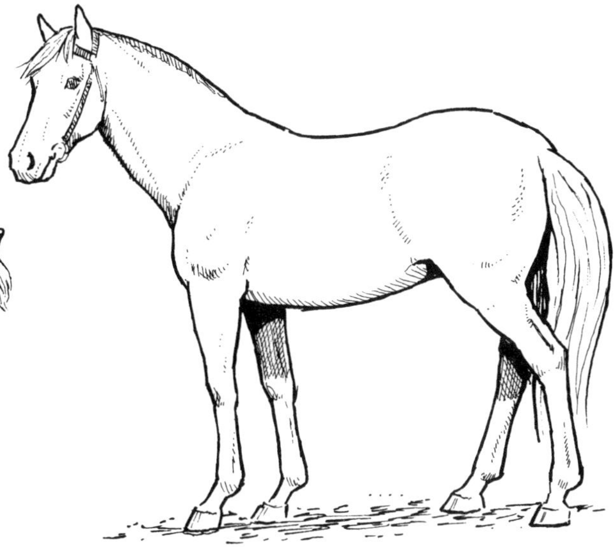

French Trotter
216

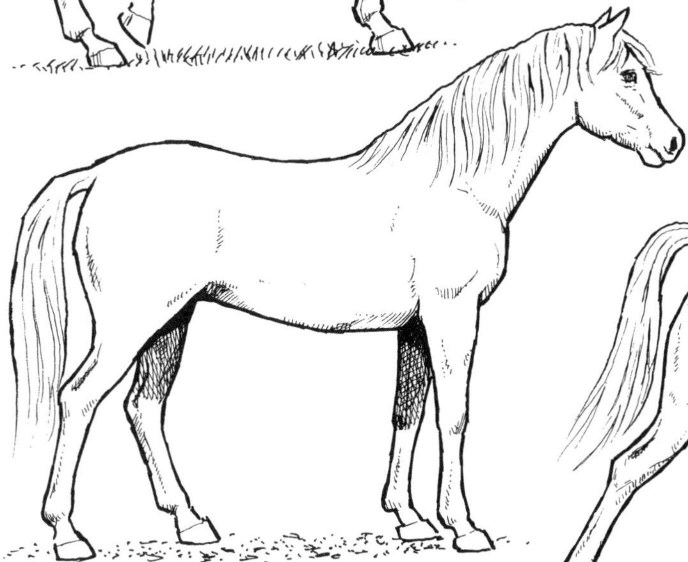

Anglo Arab
217

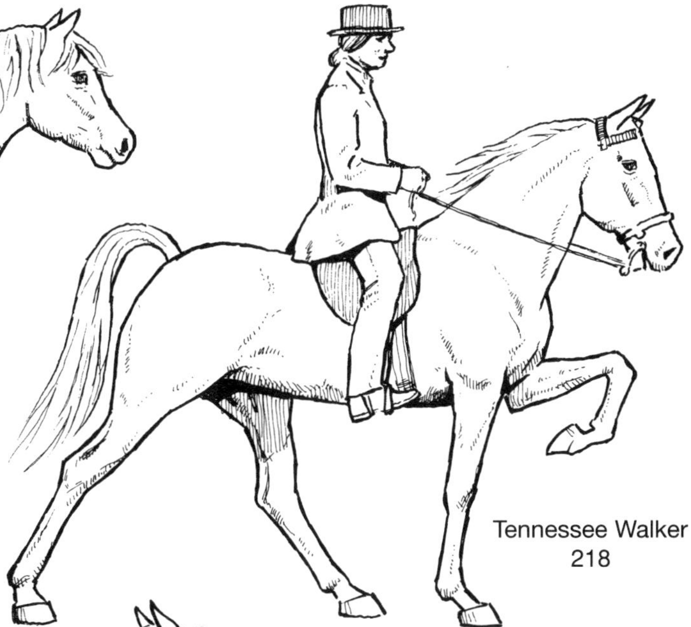

Tennessee Walker
218

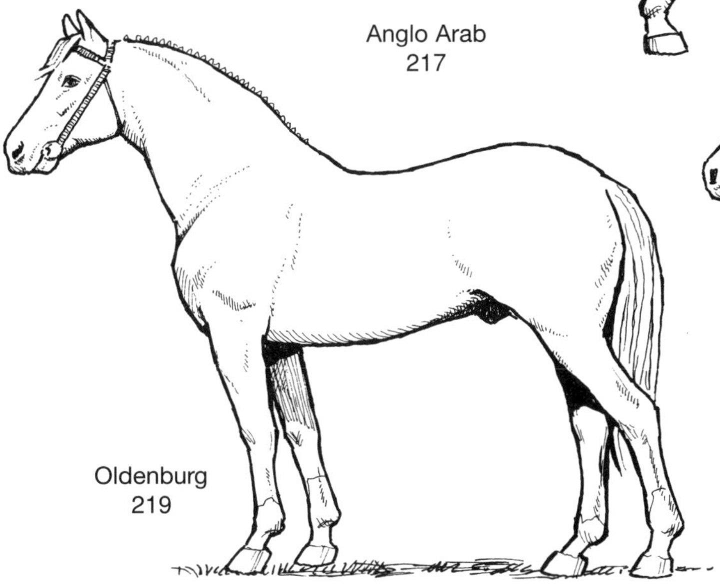

Oldenburg
219

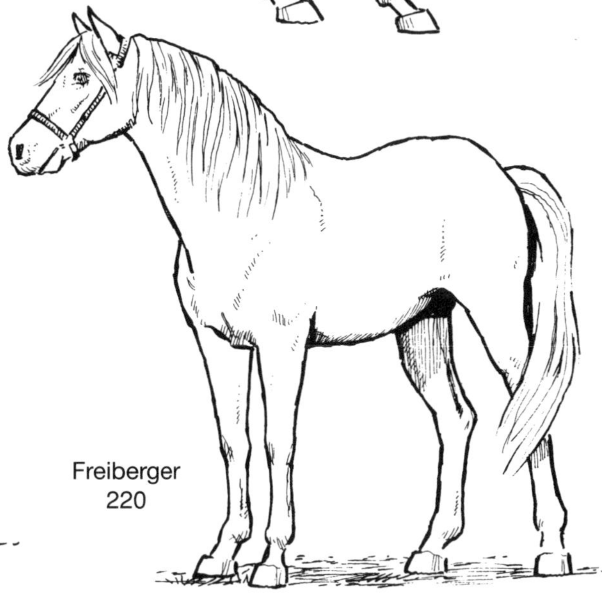

Freiberger
220

Sport Horses

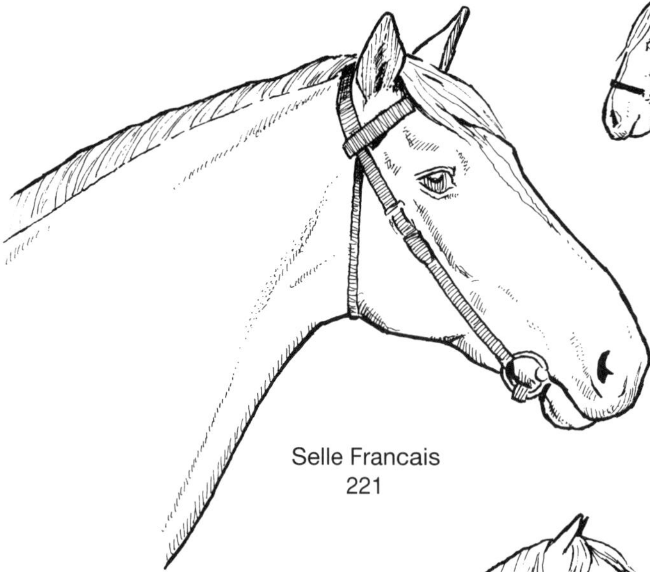

Selle Francais
221

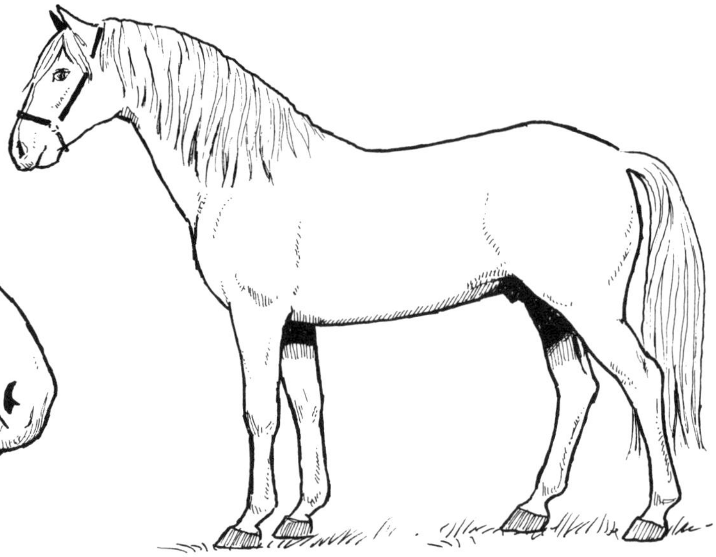

Palomino
222

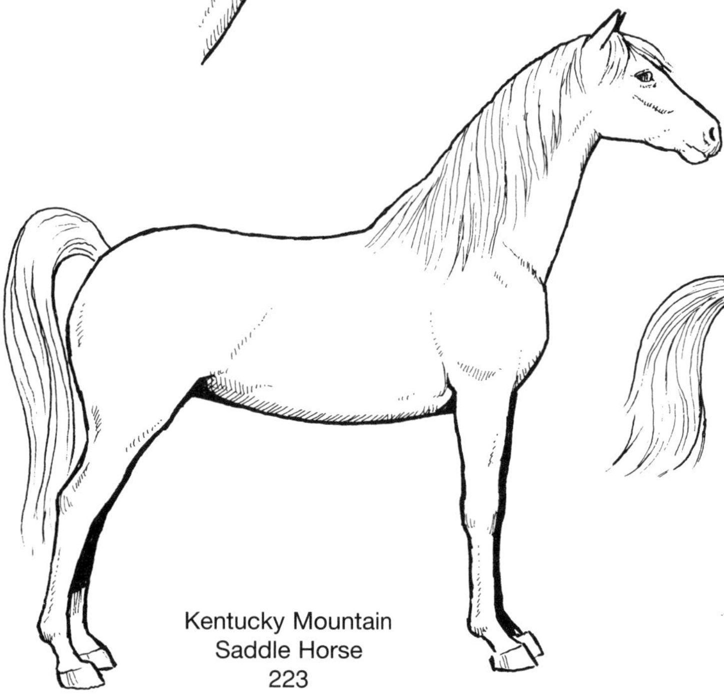

Kentucky Mountain
Saddle Horse
223

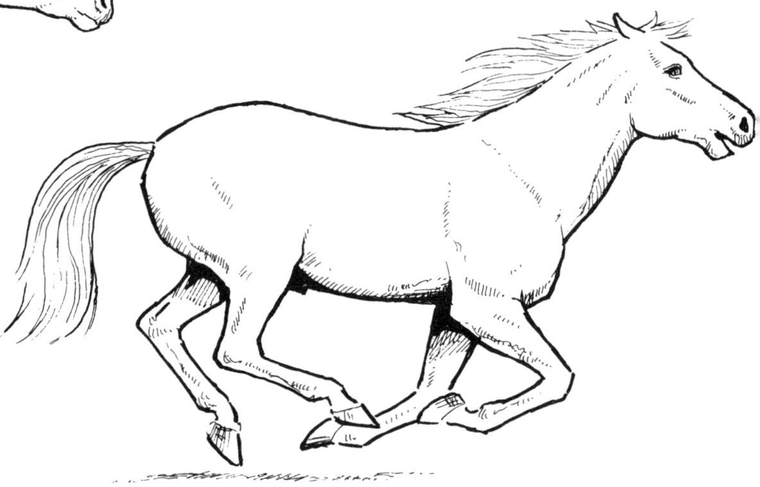

Camargue
224

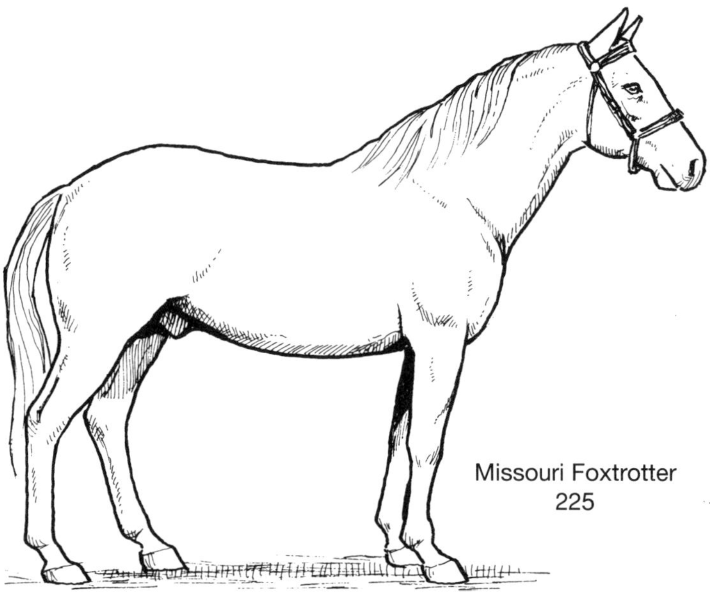

Missouri Foxtrotter
225

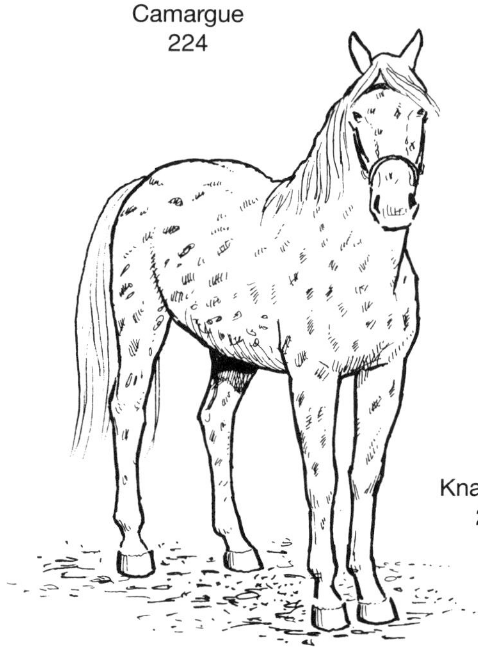

Knapstrup
226

Sport Horses

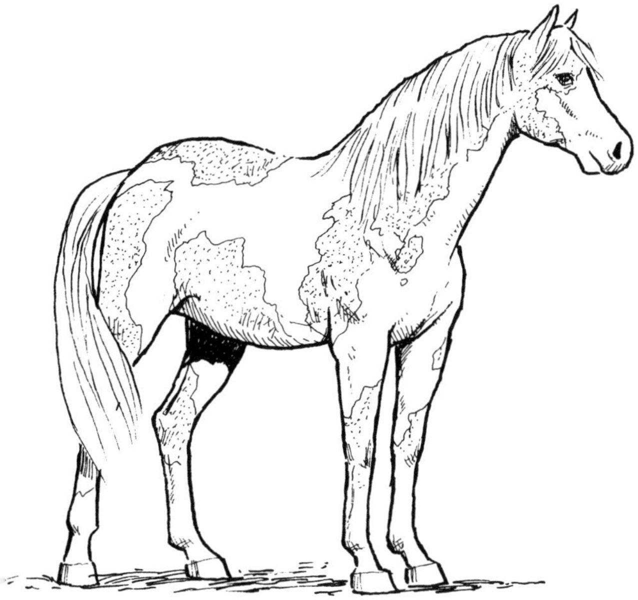

Pinto
227

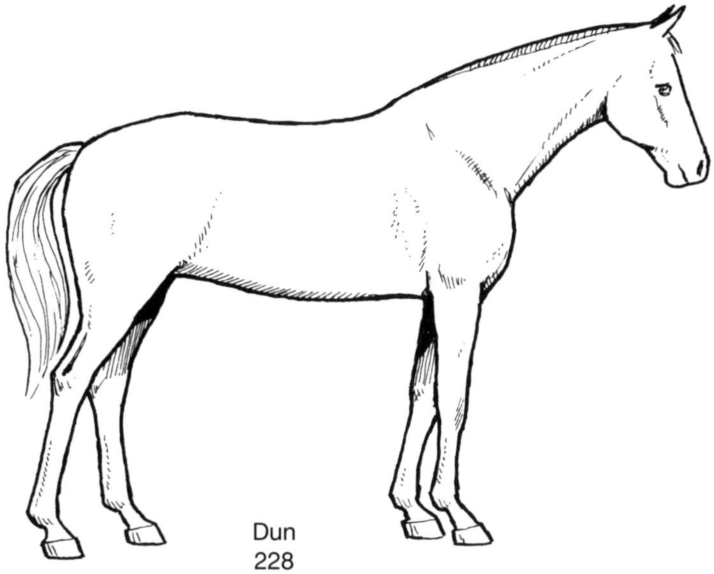

Dun
228

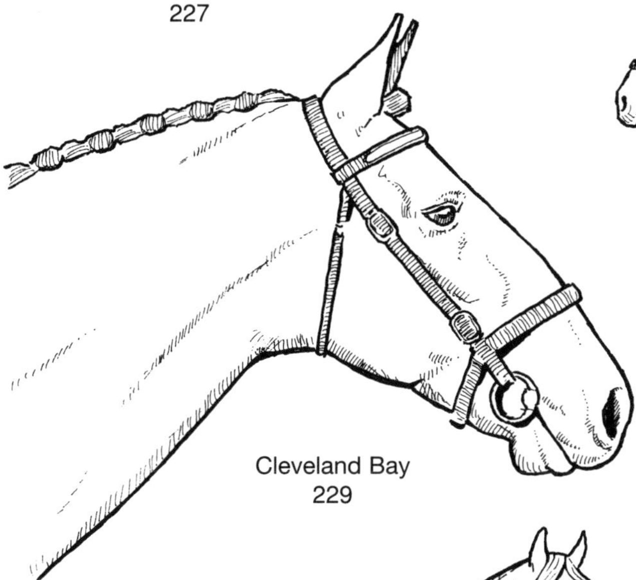

Cleveland Bay
229

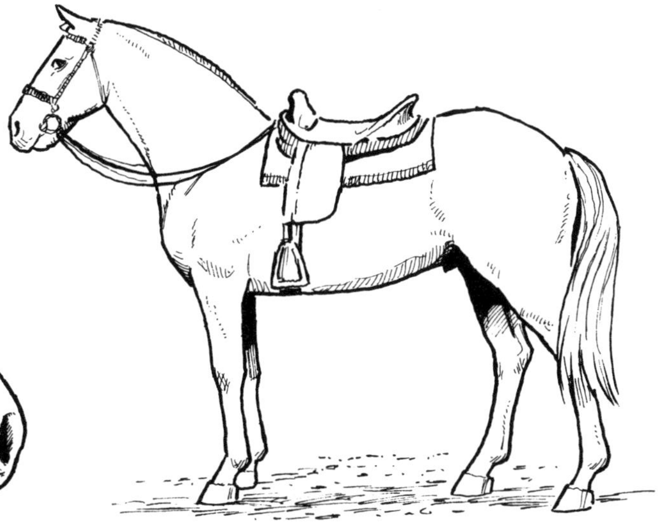

Grullo
230

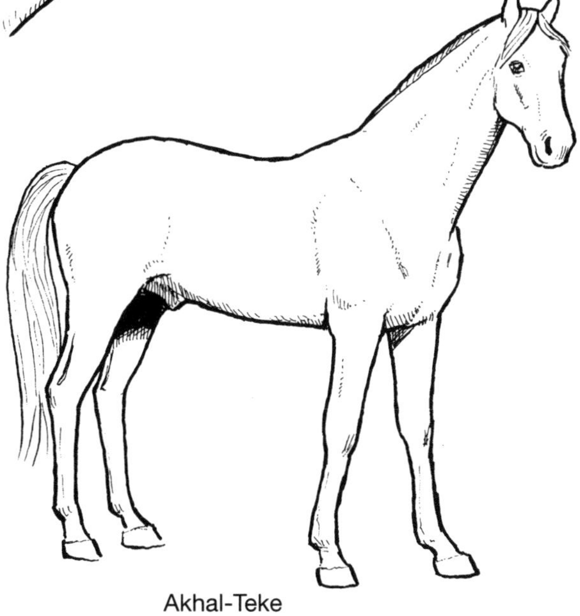

Akhal-Teke
231

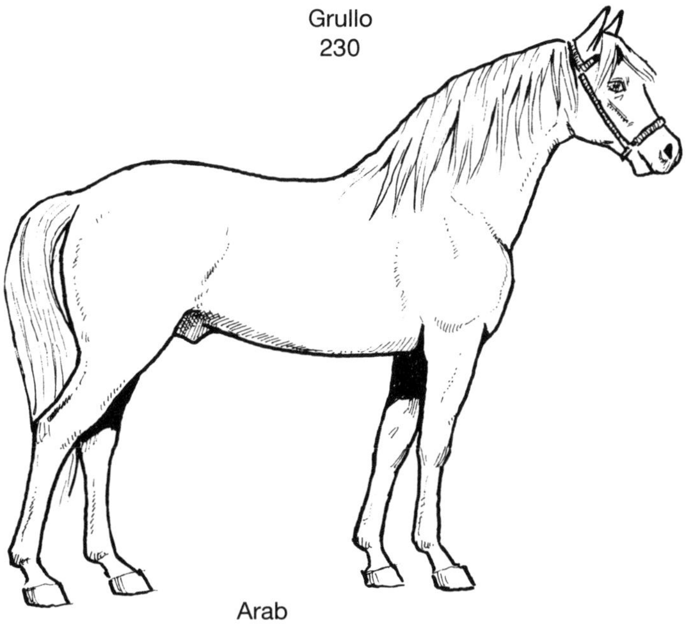

Arab
232

Work Horses

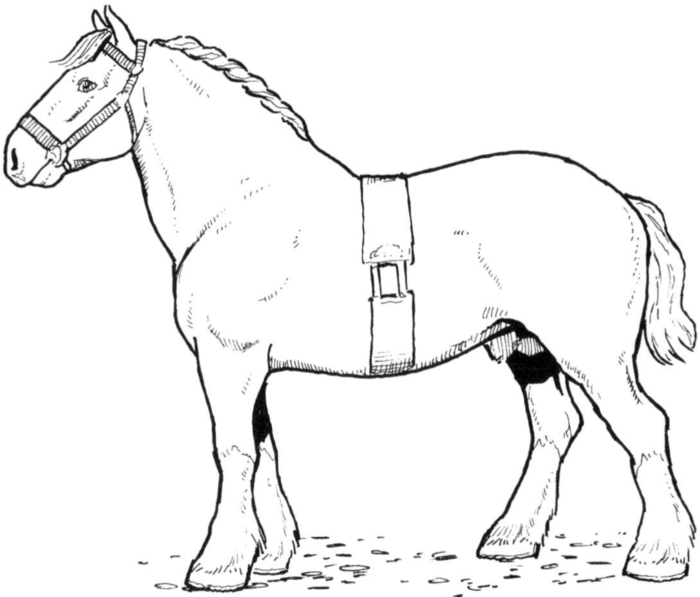

Dutch Draft
233

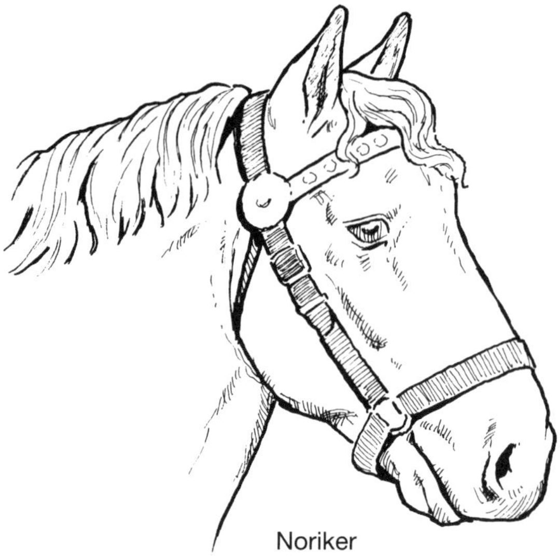

Noriker
234

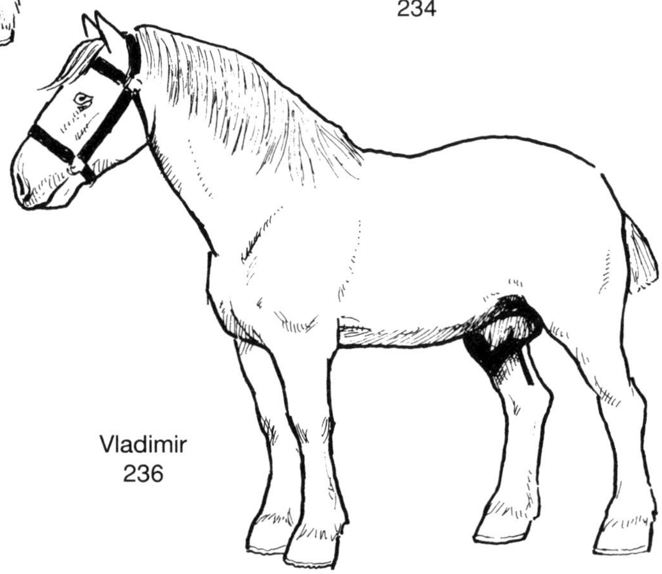

Vladimir
236

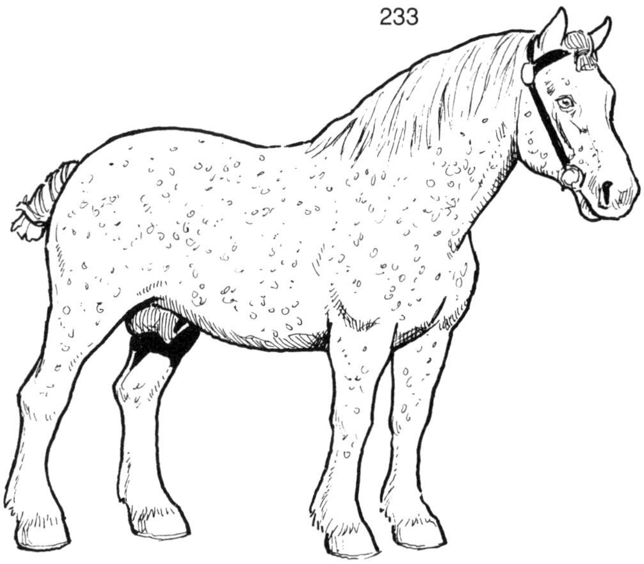

Percheron
235

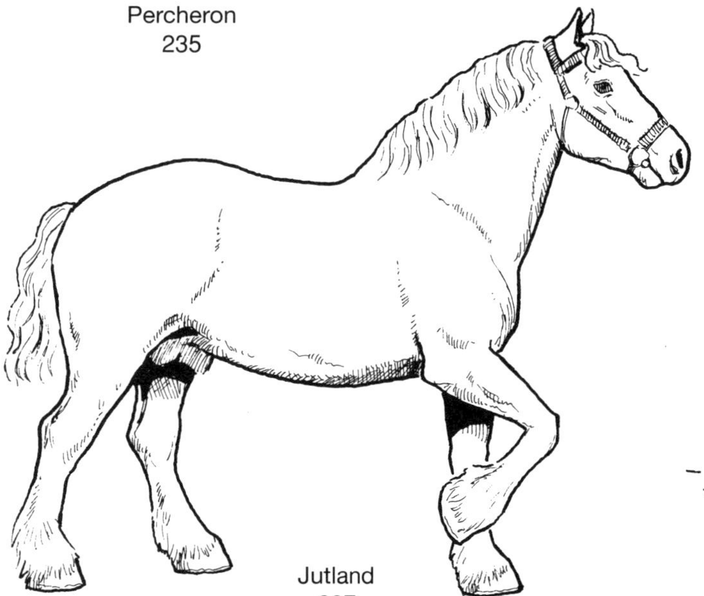

Jutland
237

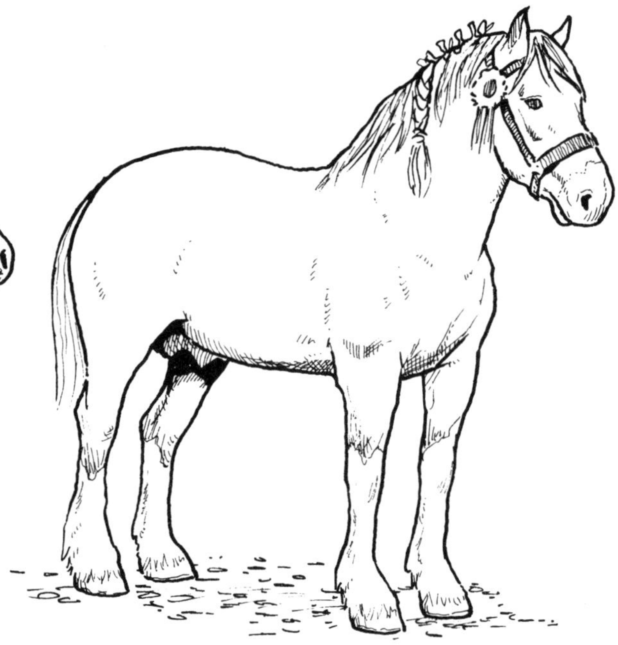

Clydesdale
238

Work Horses

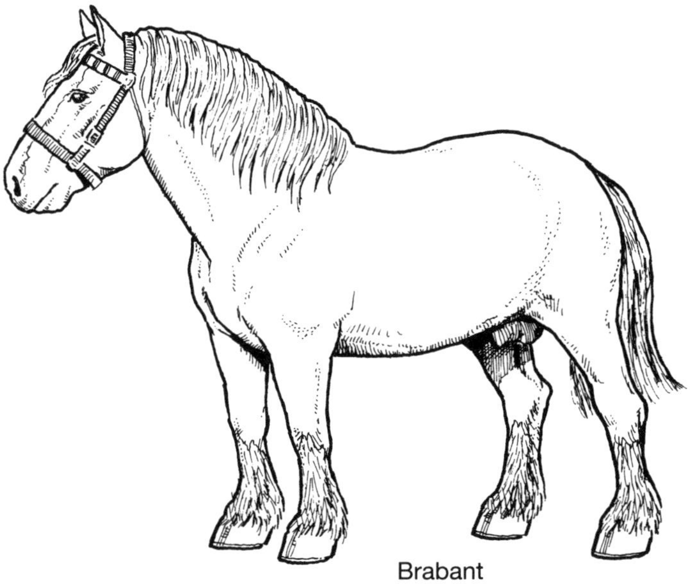

Brabant
239

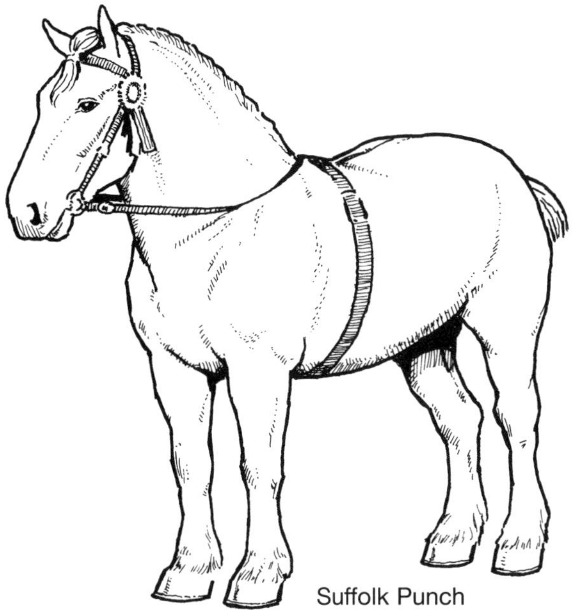

Suffolk Punch
240

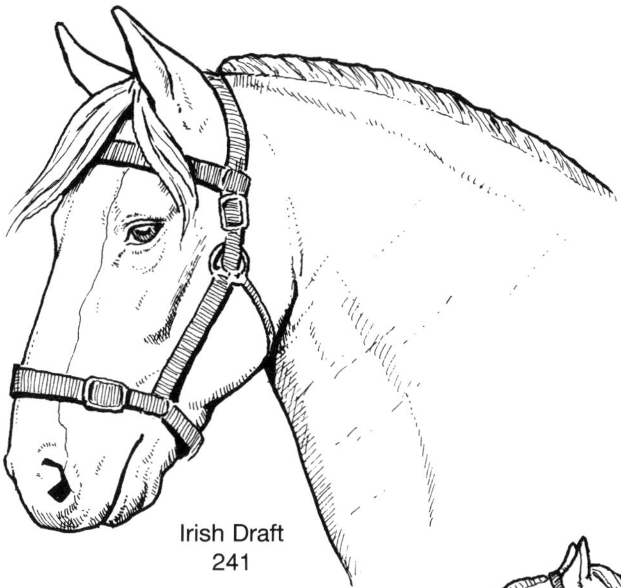

Irish Draft
241

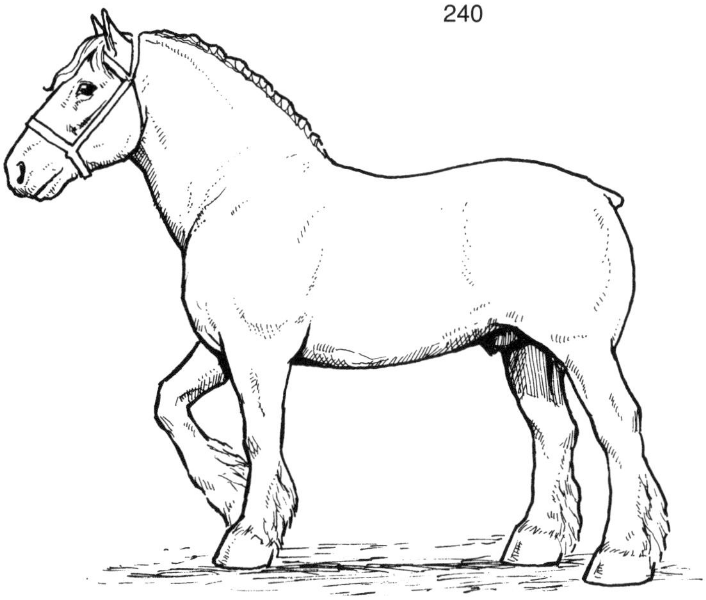

Irish Draft
242

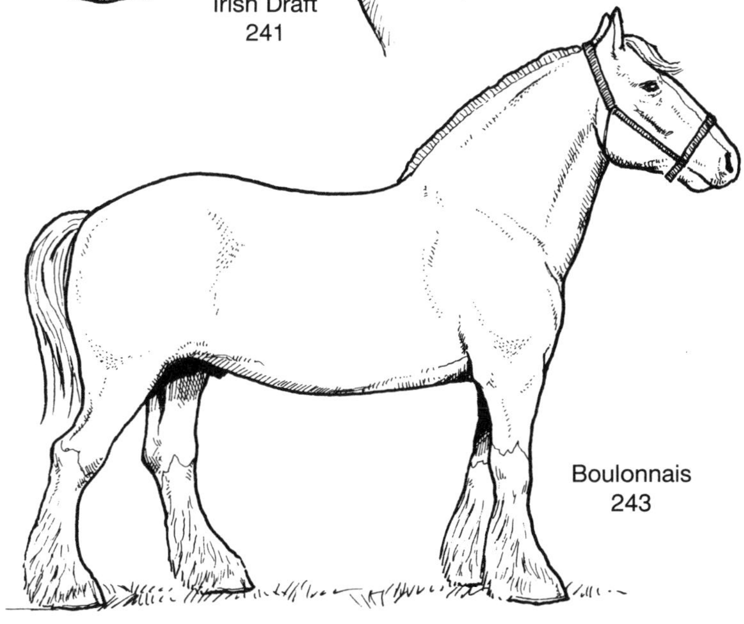

Boulonnais
243

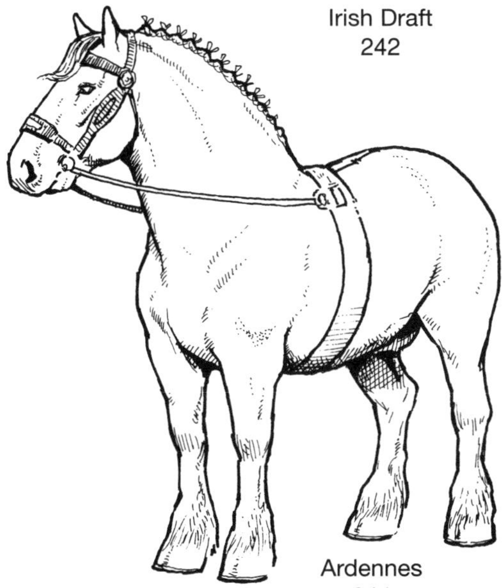

Ardennes
244

Work Horses

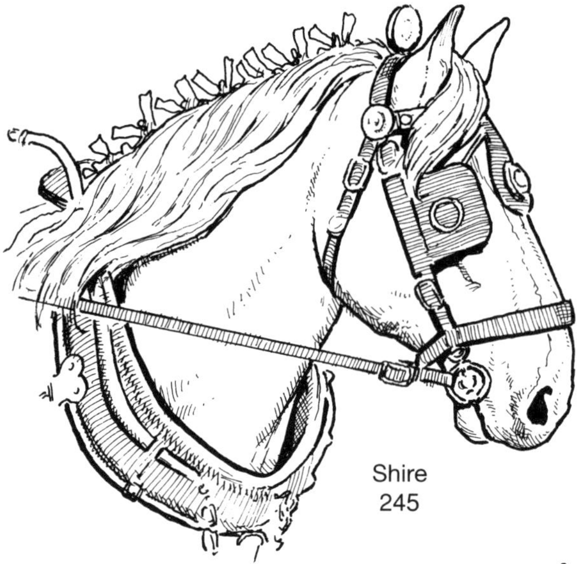

Shire
245

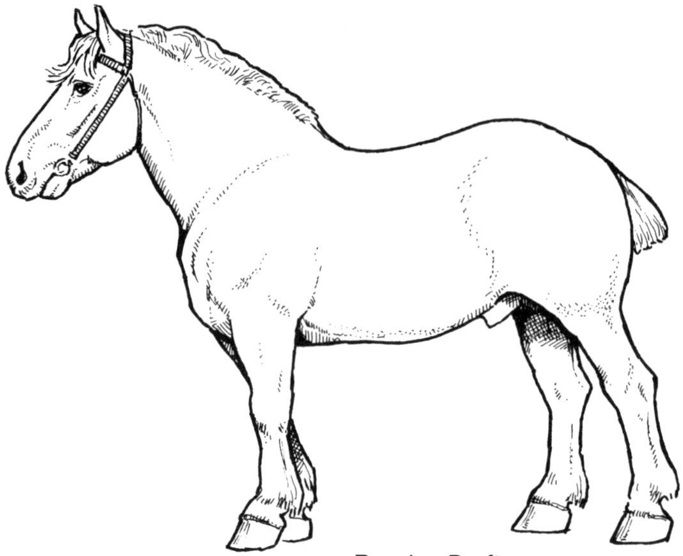

Russian Draft
246

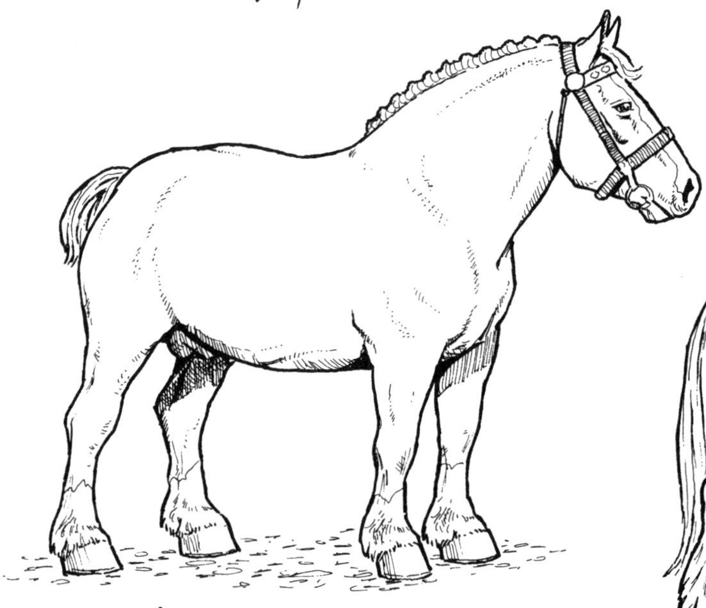

Breton
247

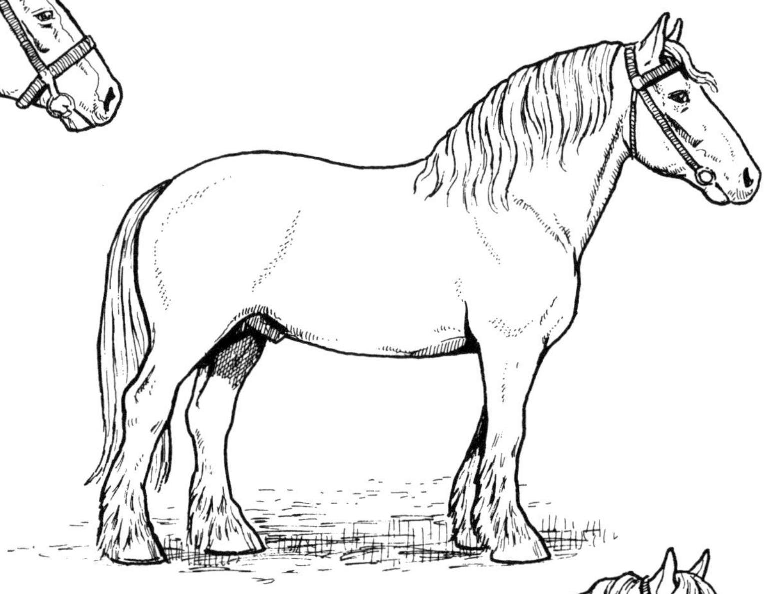

South German Cold Blood
248

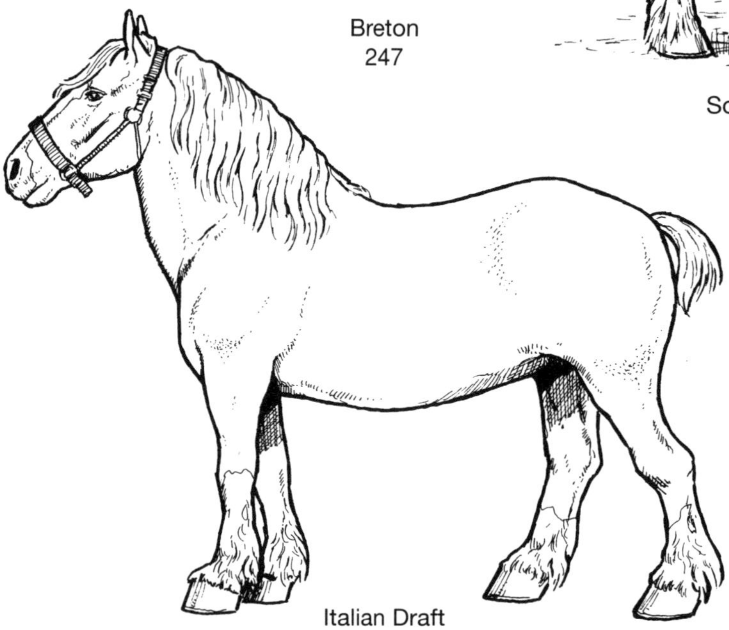

Italian Draft
249

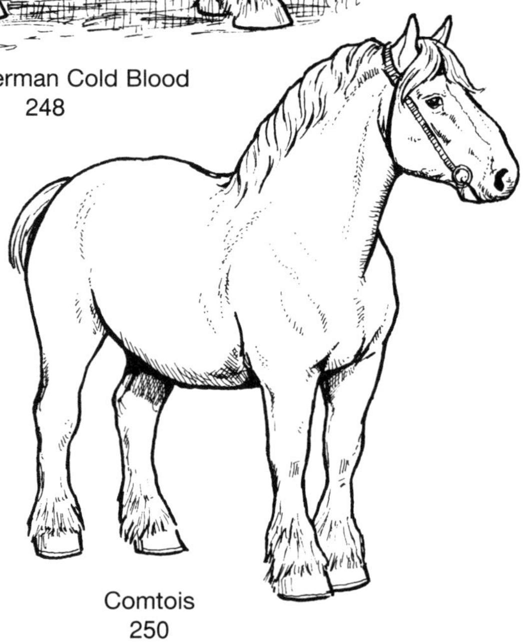

Comtois
250

Work Horses

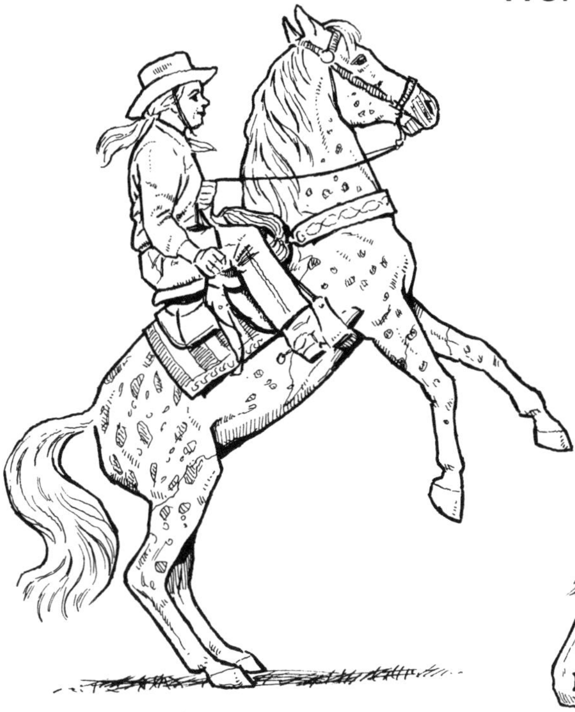

Pony of the Americas
251

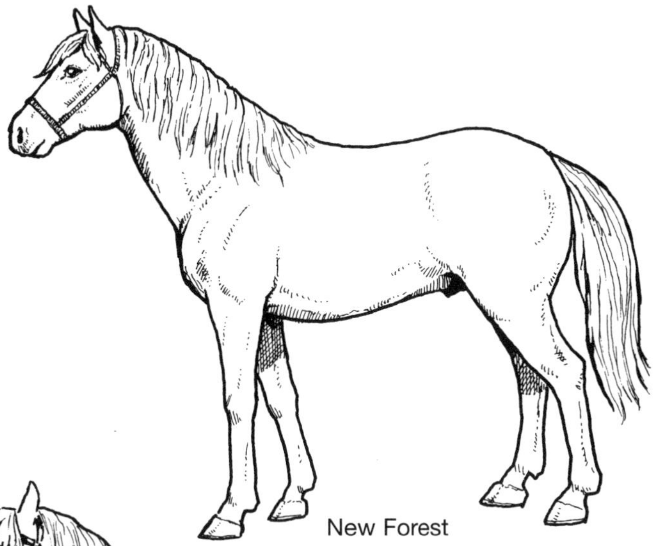

New Forest
252

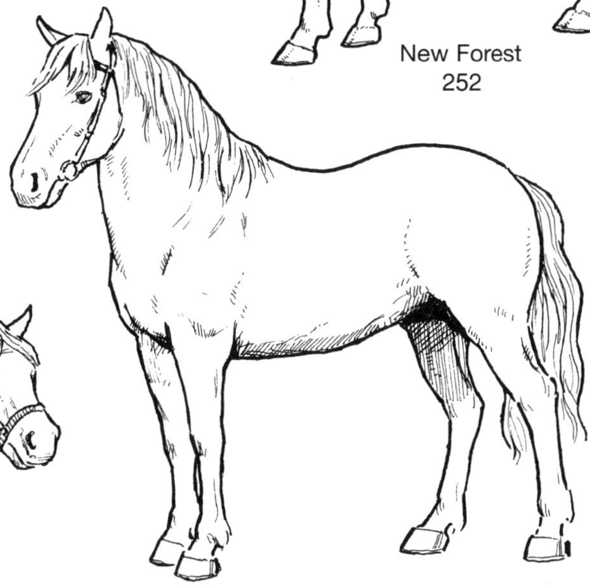

Landais
254

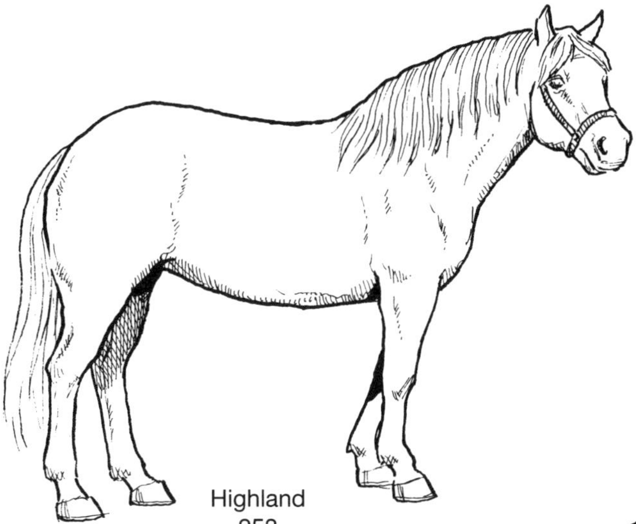

Highland
253

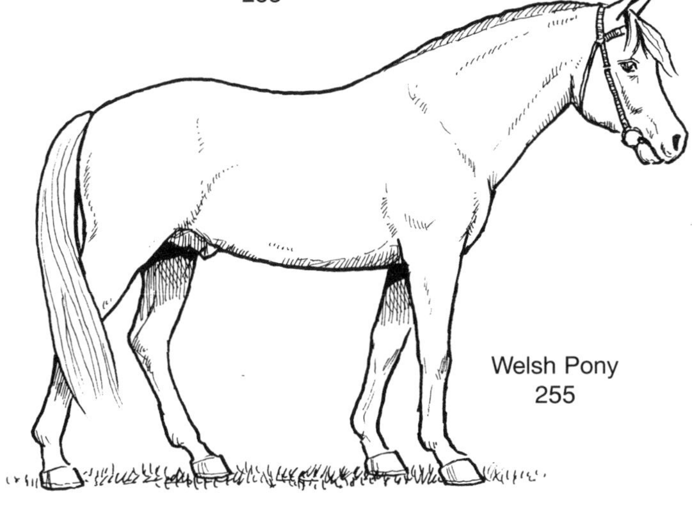

Welsh Pony
255

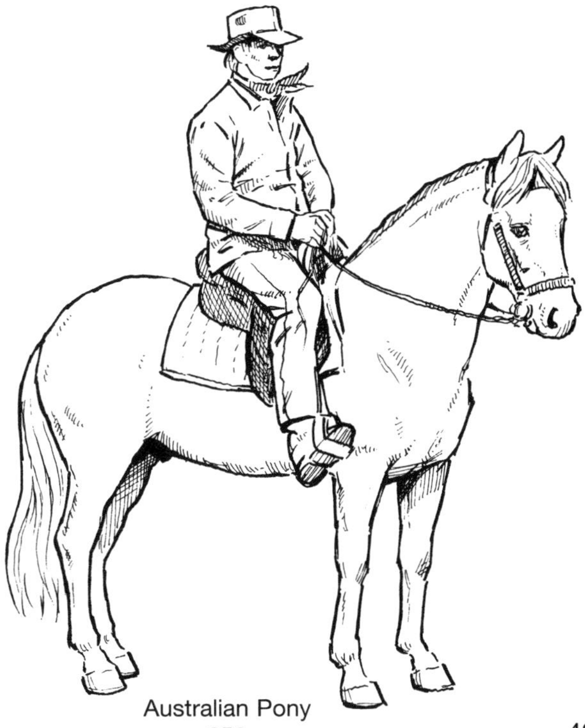

Australian Pony
256

Ponies

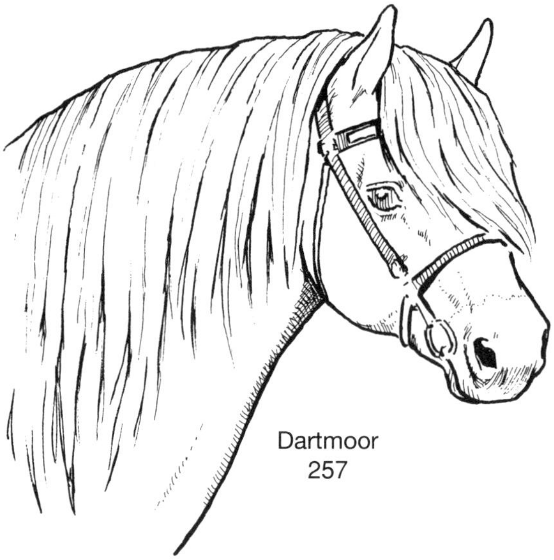

Dartmoor
257

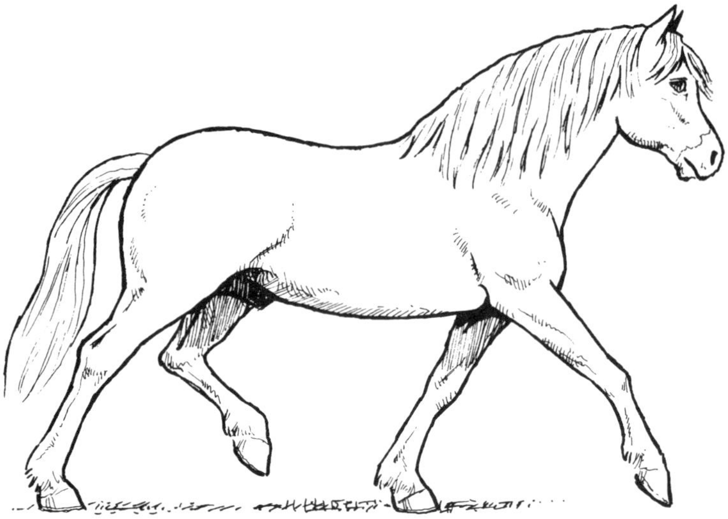

Exmoor
258

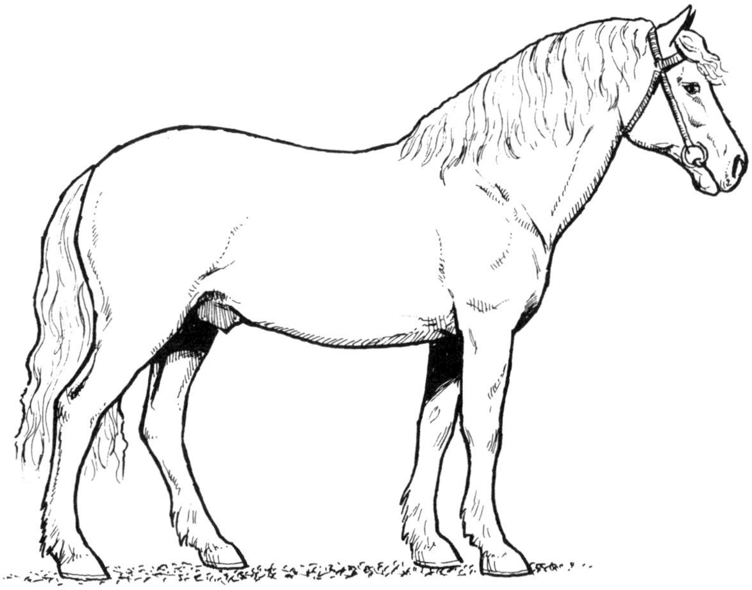

Garrano
259

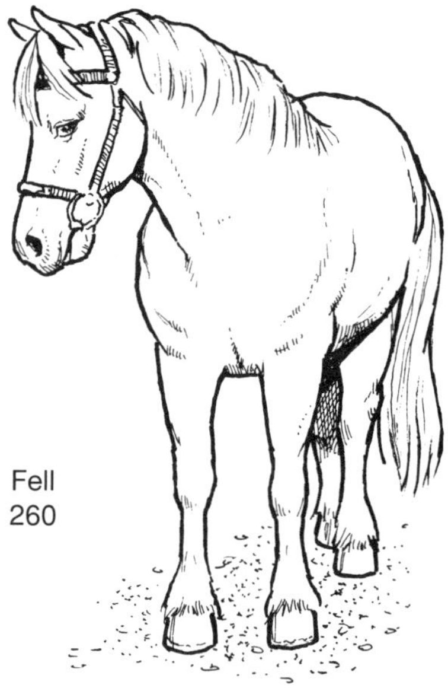

Fell
260

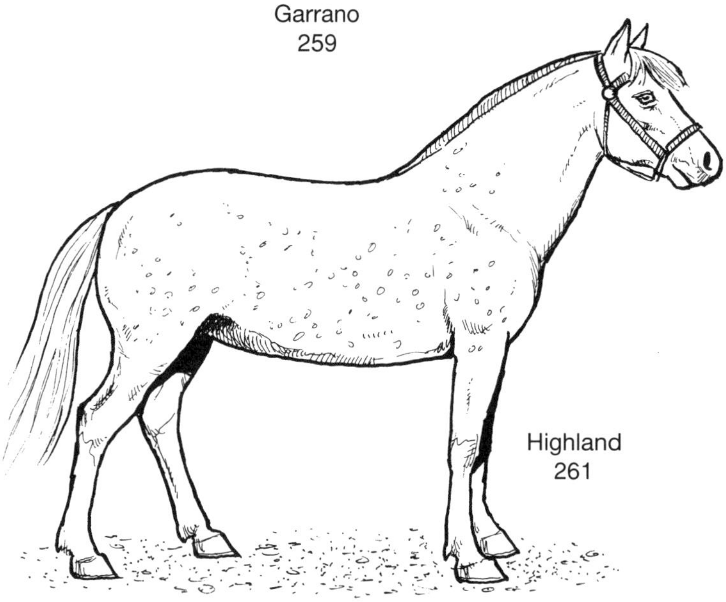

Highland
261

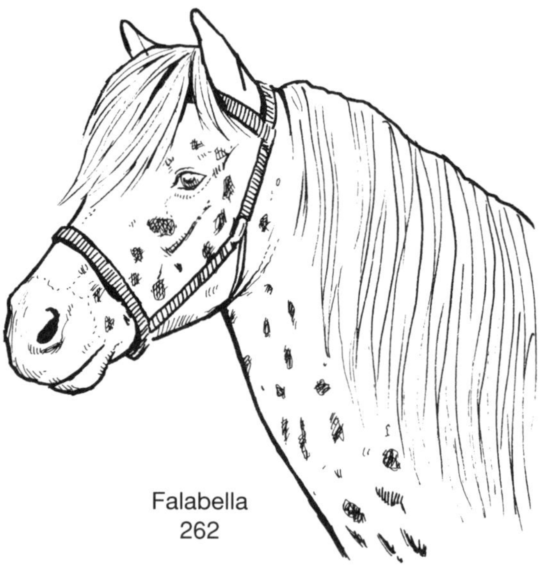

Falabella
262

Ponies

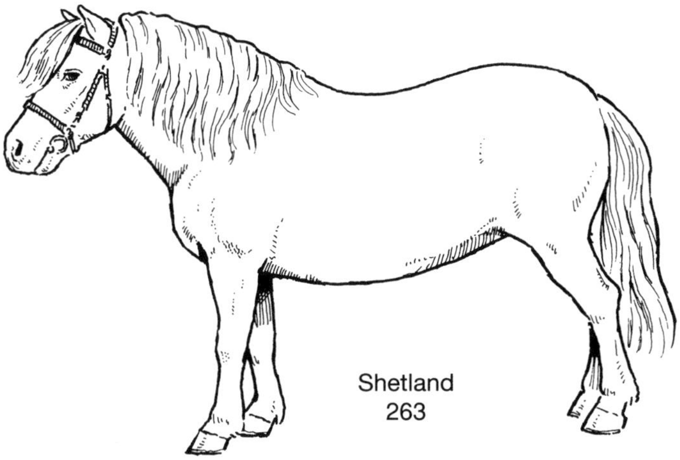

Shetland
263

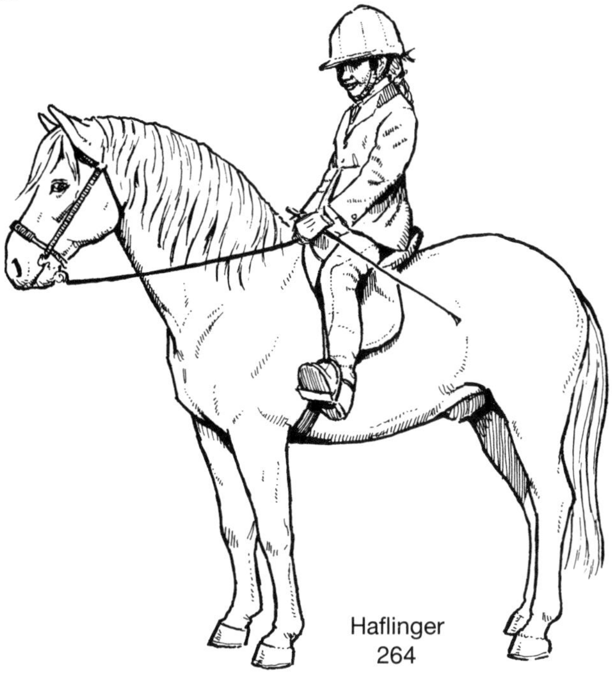

Haflinger
264

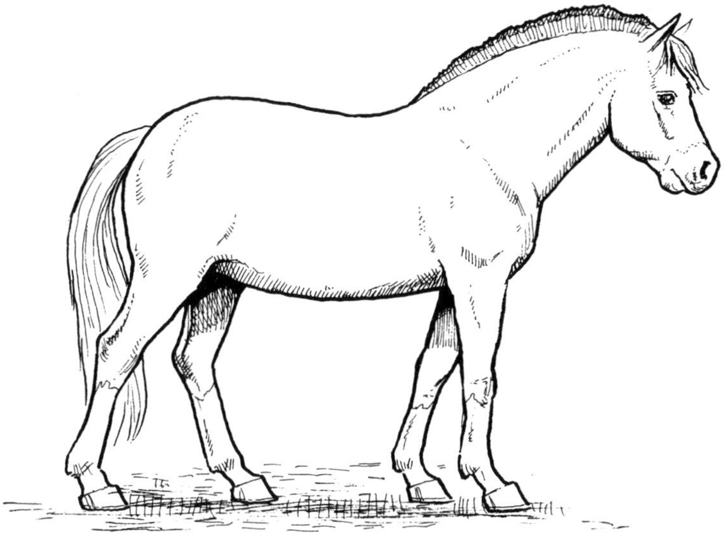

Fjord
265

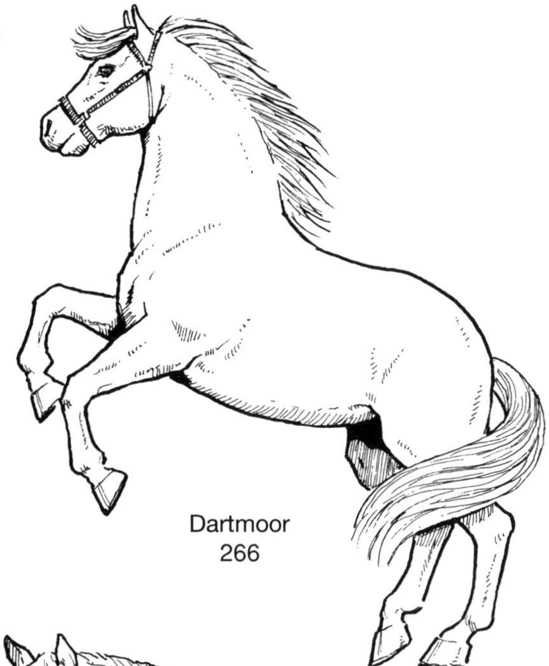

Dartmoor
266

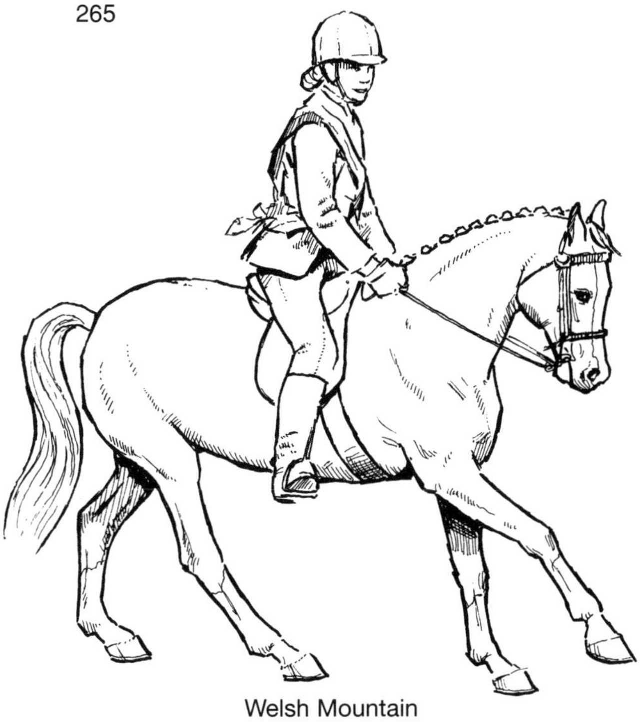

Welsh Mountain
267

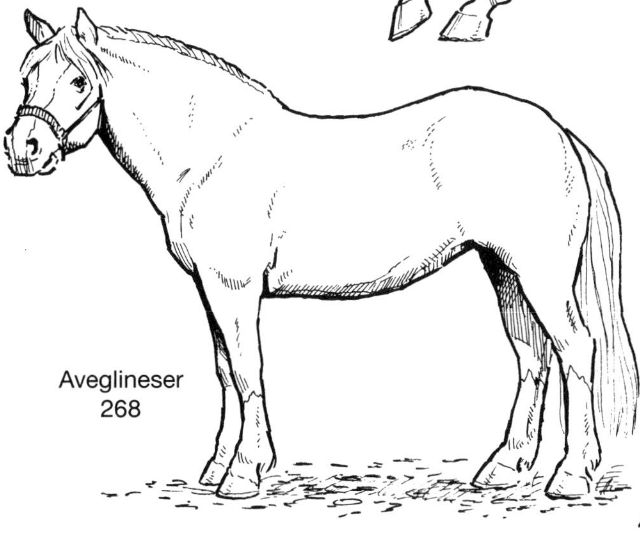

Aveglineser
268

Ponies

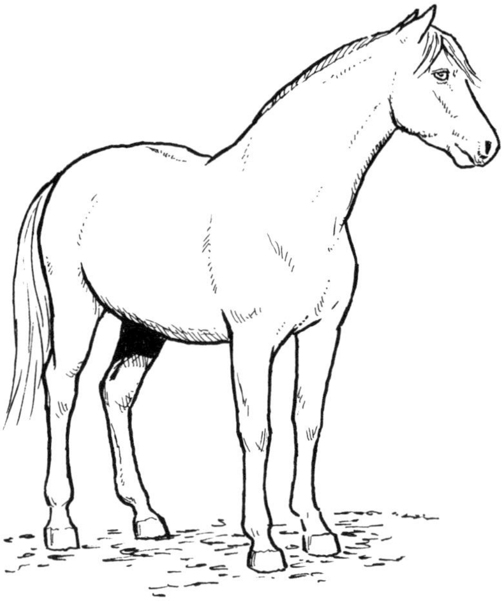

Sorraia
269

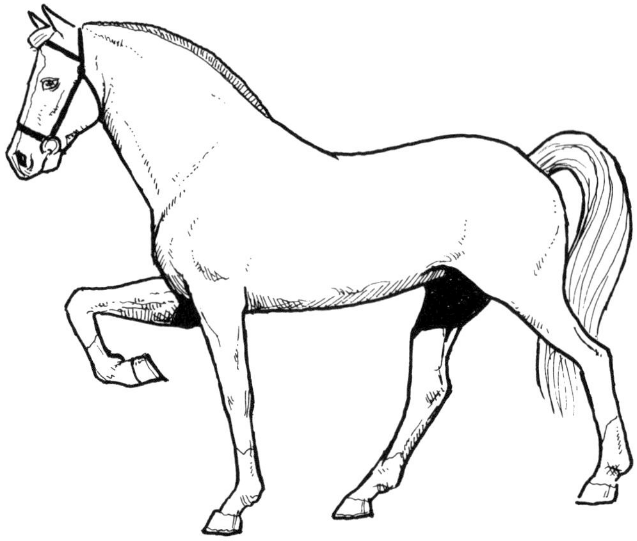

Hackney
270

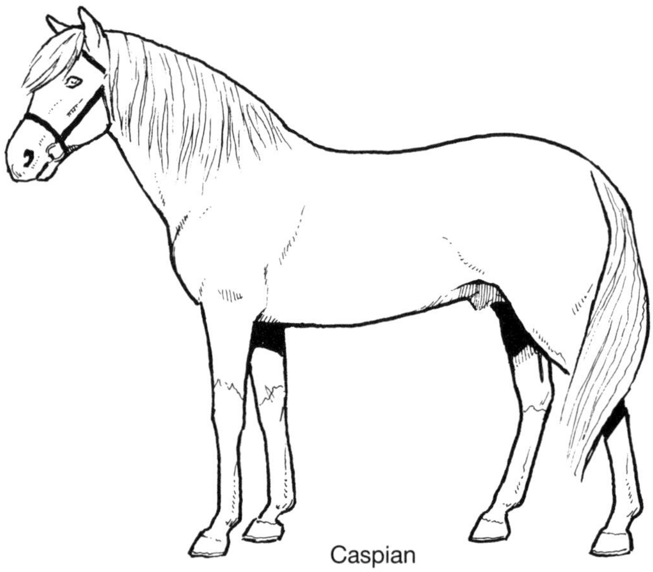

Caspian
271

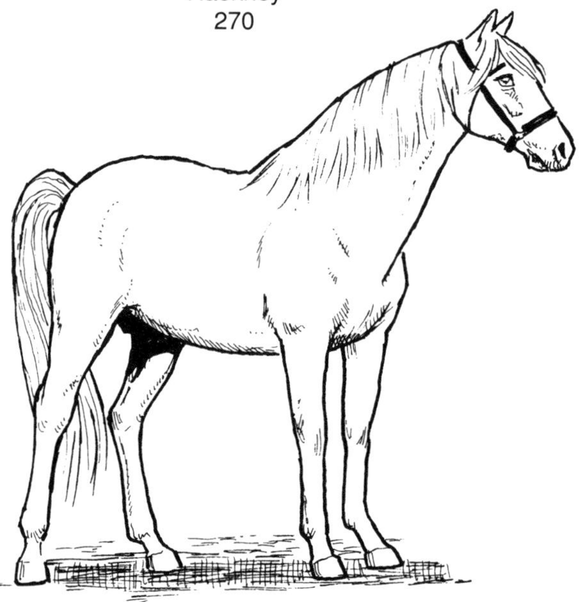

American Shetland
272

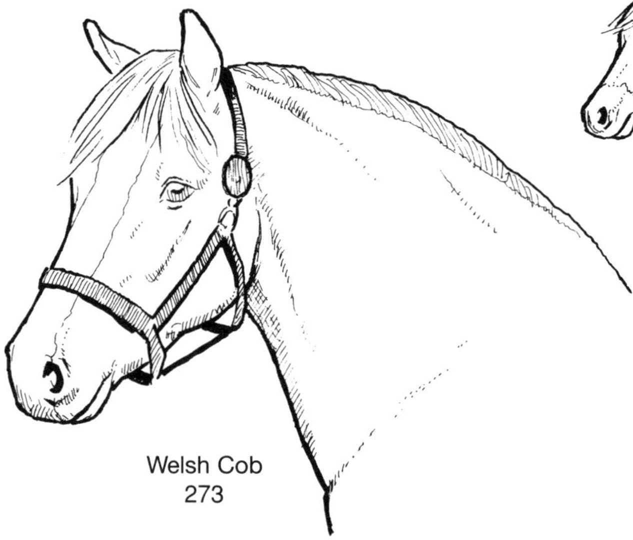

Welsh Cob
273

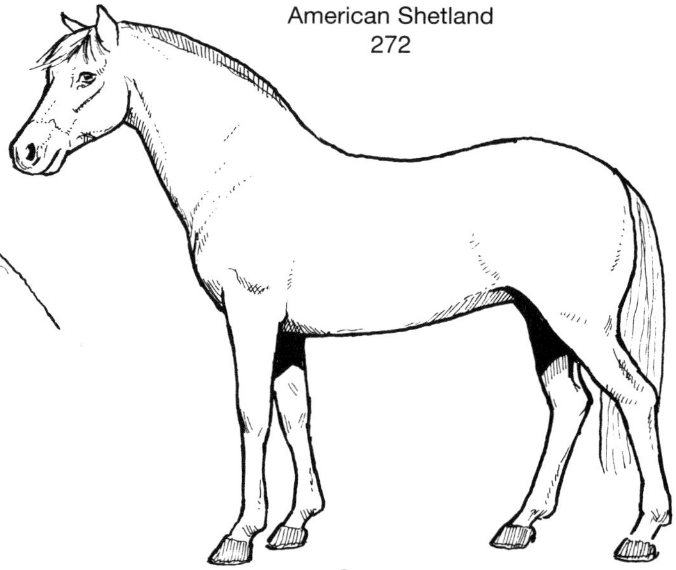

Connemara
274

Anatomy

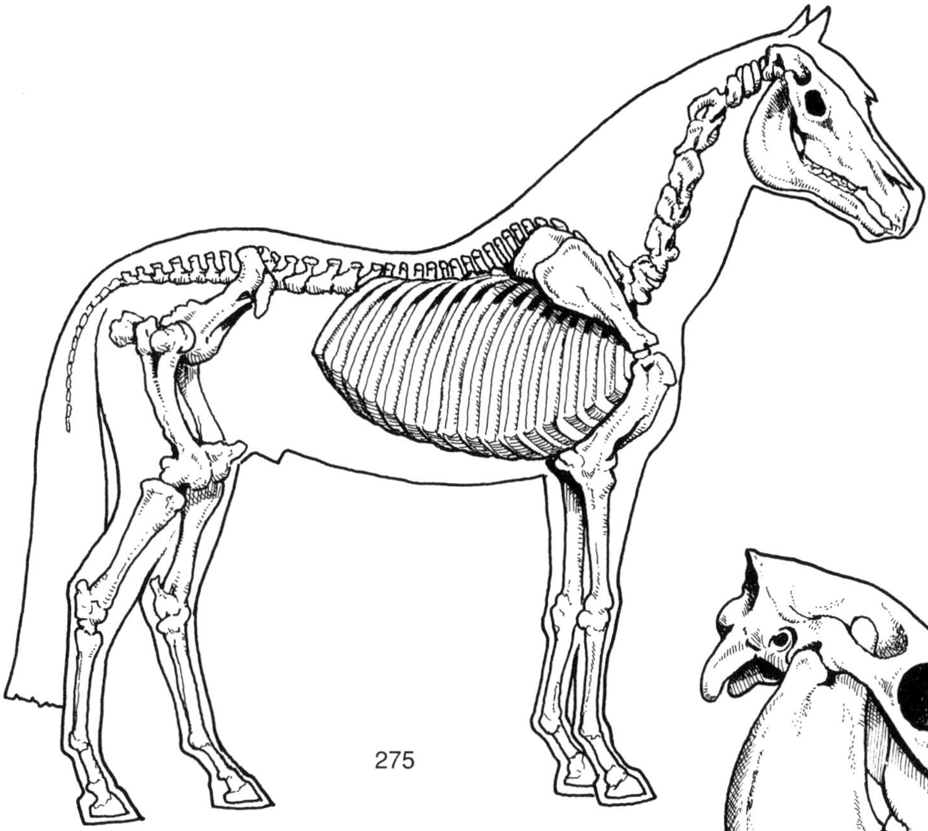

275

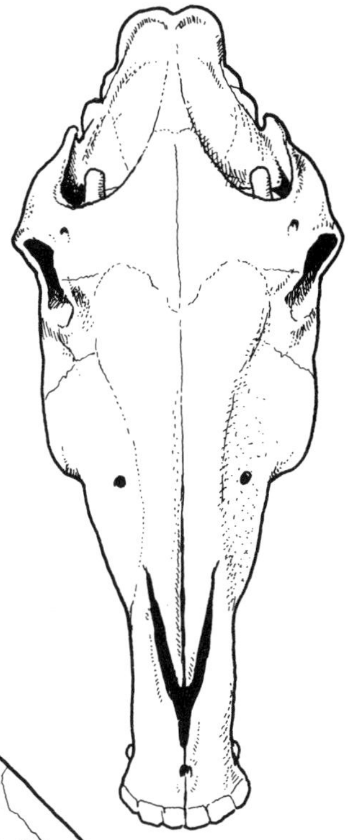

skull
276

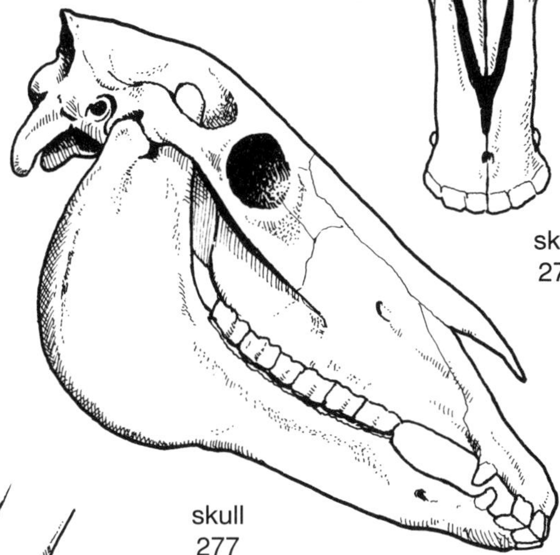

skull
277

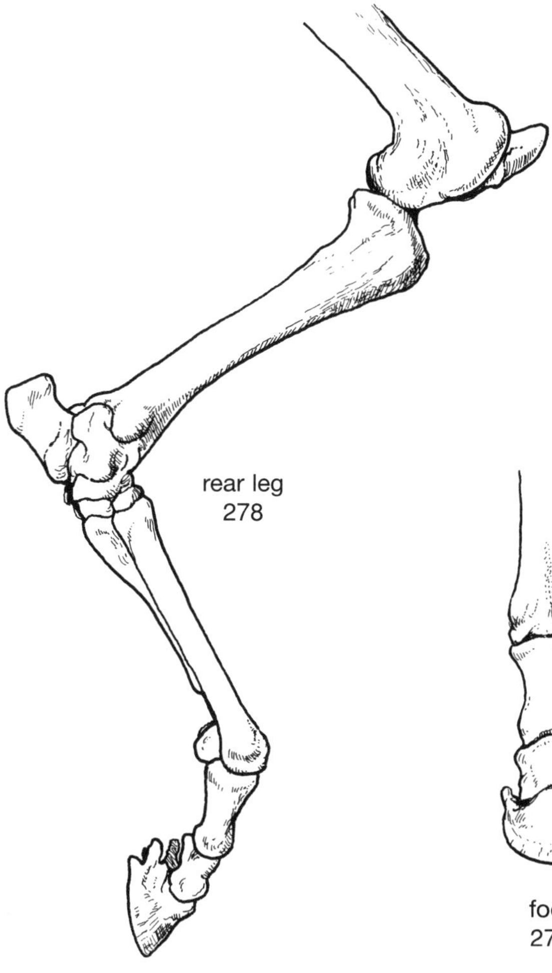

rear leg
278

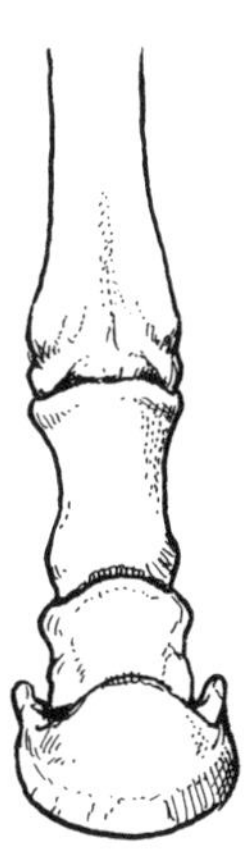

foot
279

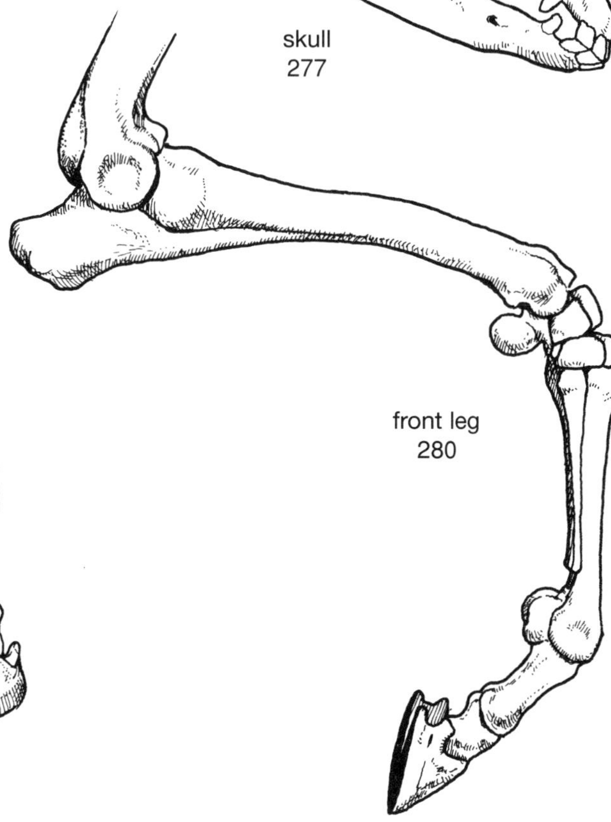

front leg
280

Anatomy

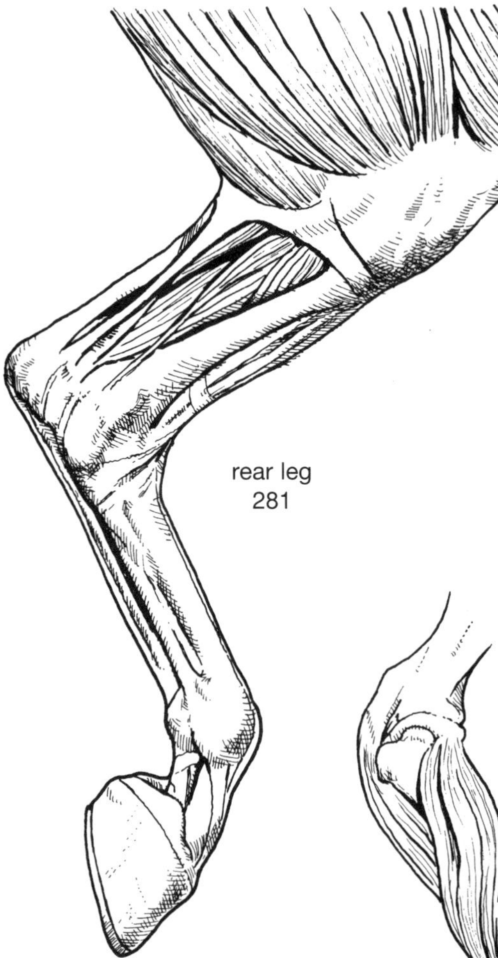

rear leg
281

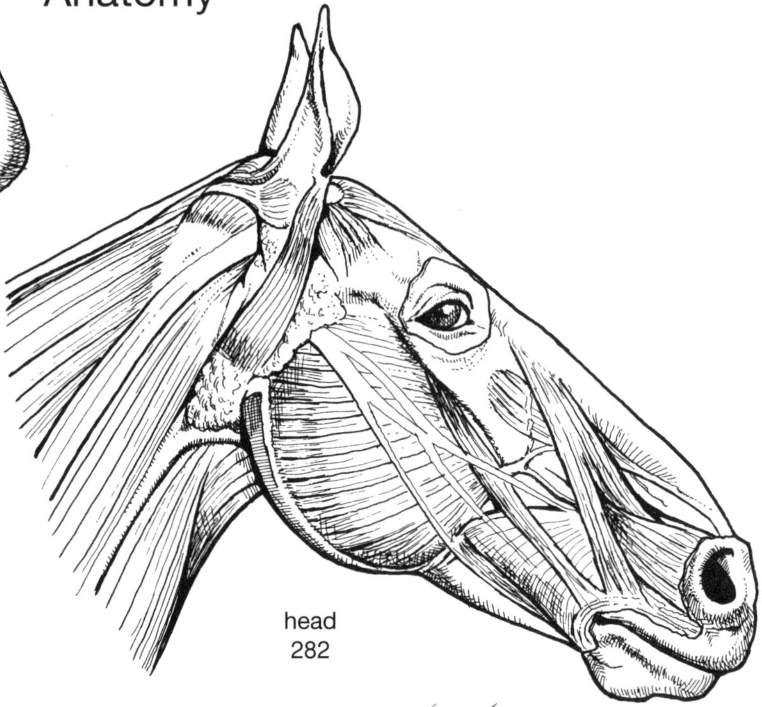

head
282

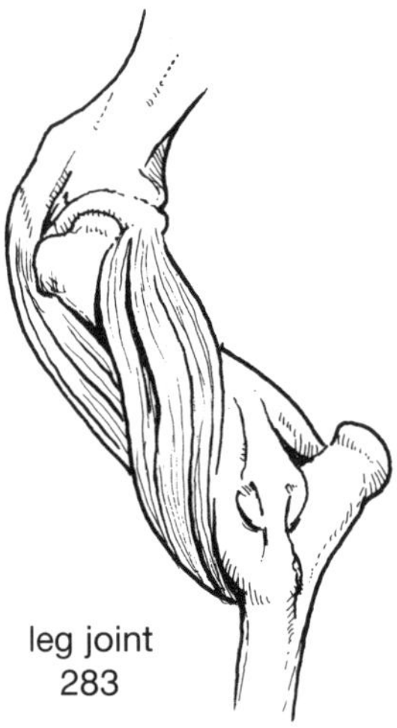

leg joint
283

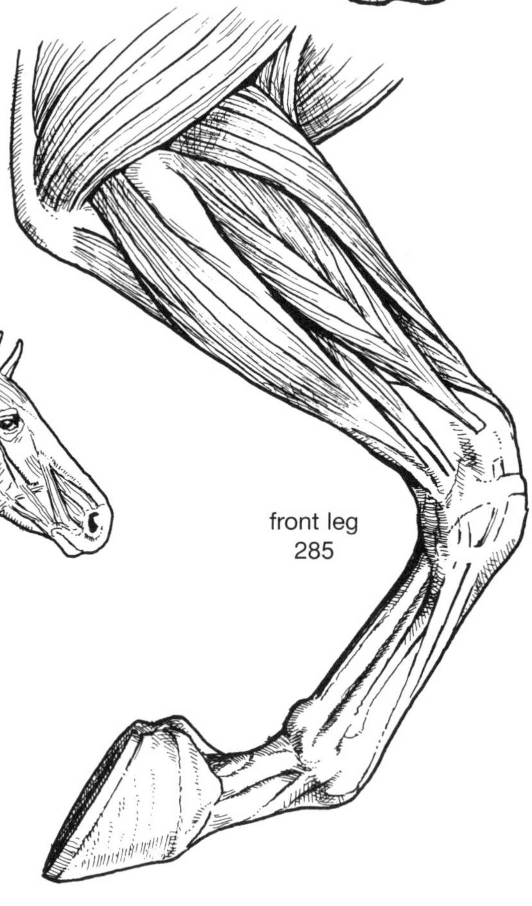

front leg
285

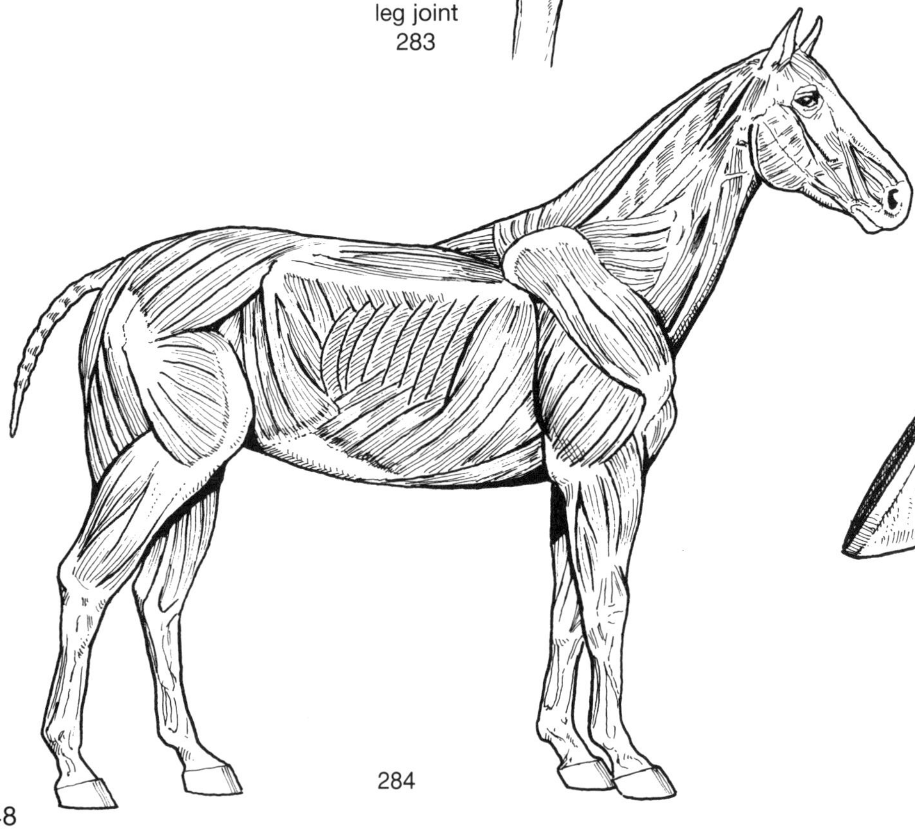

284